ANCIENT

MODERN SU

ʎ

ANCIENT BELIEFS AND
MODERN SUPERSTITIONS

*

Martin Lings

This edition published by
Archetype
Chetwynd House
Bartlow
Cambridge CB21 4PP, UK

ISBN 978 1 901383 02 7

British Library Cataloguing in Publication Data
A catalogue record for this book is available from
the British Library

Typeset by Colin Etheridge
Printed and bound in Great Britain by
TJ International Ltd, Padstow, Cornwall

Preface

A peculiar feature of our times is the enormous importance which is attached not only in politics but now also even in religion to the consideration of whether this or that is 'in keeping with the spirit of modernity'. The cult of our day, which is really the cult of ourselves, produces a general frame of mind as unfavourable to religion as anything could be, an inflation of the soul which is altogether incompatible with true intelligence, let alone spirituality.

This book is an attempt to restore the balance. There could be no point, however, in doing justice to the past at the expense of justice to the present, nor may it be denied that there are, or can be, great spiritual advantages in being alive today. But it is only possible to appreciate these and to benefit from them fully on condition that we see our age as it truly is, and not as its idolaters make it out to be. The modern world is full of ironies, and not the least of them is that the most ardent champions of the twentieth century, and now of the twenty-first, are of all men the blindest to the real assets of the times we live in.

Martin Lings

CONTENTS

Preface   v

1   The Past in the Light of the Present   1

2   The Rhythms of Time   15

3   The Present in the Light of the Past   24

4   Freedom and Equality   40

5   Intellect and Reason   51

6   The Meeting of Extremes   61

    Appendix One   69

    Appendix Two   74

CONTENTS

ONE

The Past in the Light of the Present

WOULD the peoples of old have changed their attitude towards their earliest ancestors if they had known all that modern scientists now know?

This is in some ways equivalent to another question: is there any real incompatibility between religion and science?—for the opinions of our forefathers were largely based on religion.

Let us take one or two examples of 'stumbling blocks', considering them in the light of both religion and science, and not in the darkness of either.

Does religion claim that prehistoric events can be dated on the basis of a literal interpretation of figures mentioned in the Old Testament, and that the approximate date of the Creation itself is 4,000 BC? It could hardly make such a claim, for 'a thousand years in Thy Sight are but as yesterday' and it is by no means always clear, when days are mentioned in sacred texts, whether they are human days or whether they are Divine Days each consisting of 'a thousand human years', that is, a period which bears no comparison with a human day.

Can science allow that the earth was created about 6,000 years ago? Clearly it cannot, for evidence of various kinds shows beyond doubt that at that date the earth and man were already old.

If science seems here to refute the letter of the Scriptures, it does not refute their spirit, for even apart from archaeological and geological evidence there are directly spiritual reasons for preferring not to insist on the letter of Genesis chronology. This does not mean that our mediaeval ancestors, many if not most of whom did accept a literal interpretation, were less spiritual or less intelligent than ourselves—far from it. But although, as we shall see later, they almost certainly had a more qualitative sense of time than we have, that is, a keener sense of its rhythms, they no doubt had less sense of time in a purely quantitative way; and it did not strike them, as it can scarcely fail to strike us, that there is something spiritually incongruous in the idea of an All-Powerful God's creation being so remarkably unsuccessful that *within a very short space of time* the Creator saw need to drown the whole human race, except for one family, in order to be able to start afresh. But even apart from questions of time, the men of the Middle Ages were too conscience-stricken to reason as we do, too overwhelmed by a sense of human responsibility—to their credit be it said. If what had happened was incongruous, not to say monstrous, all the more blame to man. This way of thinking certainly comes nearer to the truth than some more modern trends of thought do, but it does not correspond to the whole truth; and we who tend to look at the question more 'detachedly' cannot help seeing that God has *His* responsibilities also. None the less it remains for each one of us to ask himself exactly how sublime his own detachment is, always remembering that a man who is standing idly down in the plain sometimes has a better view of certain aspects of a mountain than have those who are actually climbing it.

Whatever answers we may give to this question, the fact remains that our sense of what is to the Glory of God and what is not fits in less well, as regards bare chronology, with the perspective of mediaeval Christendom than it does with the perspective of the Ancient World, according to which it is only after having granted mankind many thousands of years of spiritual well-being that God has allowed it to pass through a relatively short period of decay, or in other words allowed it to 'grow old'. In any case this more ancient perspective cannot lightly be brushed aside. Its basis, the tradition of the four ages of the cycle of time which the Greeks and Romans named the Golden, Silver, Bronze and Iron Ages, is not merely European but is also to be found in Asia, among the Hindus, and in America among the Red Indians. According to Hinduism, which has the most explicit doctrine on this subject, the Golden Age was by far the longest; the ages became increasingly shorter as they were less good, the shortest and worst being the Dark Age, which corresponds to the Iron Age. But even this last and shortest age, the age we live in, stretches back more than 6,000 years into the past. What modern archaeologists call 'the Bronze Age' bears no relation to the third age of the four, and what they call 'the Iron Age' merely happens to coincide with a fraction of the fourth age.

The ancient and worldwide tradition of the four ages does not contradict the Book of Genesis, but, like the evidence of science, it does suggest an allegorical rather than a literal interpretation. It suggests, for example, that certain names indicate not merely single individuals but whole eras of prehistory, and that the name Adam in particular may be taken as denoting not only the first man but also the whole of primordial humanity, spanning a period of many thousands of years.

*

But is it necessary for religion to maintain that at some time in the past man was created in a state of surpassing excellence, from which he has since fallen?

Without any doubt yes, for if the story of the Garden of Eden cannot be taken literally, it cannot, on the other hand, be taken as meaning the opposite of what it says.[1] The purpose of allegory is, after all, to convey truth, not falsehood. Besides, it is not only Judaism, Christianity and Islam which tell of the perfection of Primordial Man and his subsequent fall. The same truth, clothed in many different imageries, has come down to us out of the prehistoric past in all parts of the world. Religions are in fact unanimous in teaching not evolution but devolution.

Is this religious doctrine contrary to scientifically known facts? Must science, in order to be true to itself, maintain the theory of evolution?

In answer to this last question let us quote the French geologist

---

1. To this obvious fact Teilhard de Chardin turned a blind eye, and here lies one of the basic weaknesses of his standpoint.

Paul Lemoine, editor of Volume v (on 'Living Organisms') of the *Encyclopédie Française*, who went so far as to write in his summing up of the articles of the various contributors:

'This exposition shows that the theory of evolution is impossible. In reality, despite appearances, no one any longer believes in it . . . . . Evolution is a sort of dogma whose priests no longer believe in it, though they uphold it for the sake of their flock.'

Though undeniably exaggerated in its manner of expression—that is, as regards its sweeping implications of hypocrisy on the part of the 'priests' in question—this judgement, coming where it does, is significant in more than one respect. There is no doubt that many scientists have transferred their religious instincts from religion to evolutionism, with the result that their attitude towards evolution is sectarian rather than scientific. The French biologist Professor Louis Bounoure quotes Yves Delage, a former Sorbonne Professor of Zoology: 'I readily admit that no species has ever been known to engender another, and that there is no absolutely definite evidence that such a thing has ever taken place. None the less, I believe evolution to be just as certain as if it had been objectively proved.' Bounoure comments: 'In short, what science asks of us here is an act of faith, and it is in fact under the guise of a sort of revealed truth that the idea of evolution is generally put forward.'[1] He quotes, however, from a Sorbonne Professor of Palaeontology, Jean Piveteau, the admission that the science of facts as regards evolution 'cannot accept any of the different theories which seek to explain evolution. It even finds itself in opposition with each one of these theories. There is something here which is both disappointing and disquieting.'[2]

Darwin's theory owed its success mainly to a widespread conviction that the nineteenth-century European represented the highest human possibility yet reached. This conviction was like a special receptacle made in advance for the theory of man's subhuman ancestry, a theory which was hailed without question by humanists as a scientific corroboration of their belief in 'progress'. It was in vain that a staunch minority of scientists, during the last hundred years,

1. *Le Monde et la Vie*, November 1963.
2. *Le Monde et la Vie*, March 1964.

persistently maintained that the theory of evolution has no scientific basis and that it runs contrary to many known facts, and it was in vain that they pleaded for a more rigorously scientific attitude towards the whole question. To criticize evolutionism, however soundly, was about as effective as trying to stem a tidal wave. But the wave now shows some signs of having spent itself, and more and more scientists are re-examining this theory objectively, with the result that not a few of those who were once evolutionists have now rejected it altogether. One of these is the already quoted Bounoure; another, Douglas Dewar, writes:

'It is high time that biologists and geologists came into line with astronomers, physicists and chemists and admitted that the world and the universe are utterly mysterious and all attempts to explain them [by scientific research] have been baffled';[1] and having divided evolutionists into ten main groups (with some subdivisions) according to their various opinions as to what animal formed the last link in the chain of man's supposedly 'pre-human' ancestry, opinions which are all purely conjectural[2] and mutually contradictory, he says: 'In 1921 Reinke wrote: "The only statement, consistent with her dignity, that science can make [with regard to this question] is to say that she knows nothing about the origin of man." Today this statement is as true as it was when Reinke made it.'[3]

If science knows nothing about the origins of man, she knows much about his prehistoric past. But this knowledge—to revert to our opening question—would have taught our ancestors little or nothing that they did not already know, except as regards chronology, nor would it have caused any general change in their attitude. For in looking back to the past, they did not look back to a complex civilization but to small village settlements with a minimum of social organization; and beyond these they looked back to men who lived without houses, in entirely natural surroundings, without books,

---

1. *The Transformist Illusion* (Preface), Sophia Perennis, Ghent, NY, 1995. For a review of this book, see Appendix One.

2. Because 'no evolutionist who values his reputation will name *any known fossil* and say that, while not human, it is an ancestor of *Homo sapiens*' p. 114.

3. p. 294.

without agriculture, and in the beginning even without clothes. It would be true then to say that the ancient conception of early man, based on sacred scriptures and on age-old traditional lore handed down by word of mouth from the remote past, was scarcely different, as regards the bare facts of material existence, from the modern scientific[1] conception, which differs from the traditional one chiefly because it weighs up the same set of facts differently. What has changed is not so much knowledge of facts as the sense of values.

Until recently men did not think any the worse of their earliest ancestors for having lived in caves and woods rather than houses. It is not so long ago that Shakespeare put into the mouth of the banished Duke, living in the forest of Arden 'as they lived in the golden world':

> Here feel we but the penalty of Adam,
> The seasons' change . . .
> And this our life, exempt from public haunt,
> Finds tongues in trees, books in the running brooks,
> Sermons in stones, and good in everything.
> I would not change it.

These words can still evoke in some souls an earnest echo, an assent that is considerably more than a mere aesthetic approval; and behind Shakespeare, throughout the Middle Ages and back into the furthest historical past, there was no time when the Western world did not have its hermits, and some of them were among the most venerated men of their generation. Nor can there be any doubt that these exceptional few who lived in natural surroundings felt a

---

1. This word means what it says and is used here: (a) To exclude the bestial features which in the illustrations to so many school books are attributed to our remote ancestors. As the palaeontologist Professor E. A. Hooton remarks: 'You can, with equal facility, model on a Neanderthaloid skull the features of a chimpanzee or the lineaments of a philosopher. These alleged restorations of ancient types of man have very little, if any, scientific value, and are likely only to mislead the public.' (Quoted by Evan Shute in *Flaws in the Theory of Evolution*, Temside Press, London, Canada, 1966, p. 215.) (b) To include evidence too often passed over in silence such as that of the Castenedolo and Calaveras skulls, which point to the existence of 'men of modern type' at a period when, according to the evolutionists, *Homo sapiens* had not yet evolved. (See Dewar, ibid, pp. 117–29, and Shute, ibid, Ch. xxi).

certain benevolent pity for their brethren's servile dependence upon 'civilization'. As to the East, it has never broken altogether with the ancient sense of values, according to which the best setting for man is his primordial setting. Among the Hindus, for example, it is still an ideal—and a privilege—for a man to end his days amid the solitudes of virgin nature.

For those who can readily grasp this point of view, it is not difficult to see that agriculture, after a certain degree of development had been reached, far from marking any 'progress', became in fact 'the thin end of the wedge' of the final phase of man's degeneration. In the Old Testament narrative, this 'wedge', consisting no doubt of hundreds of human generations, is summed up in the person of Cain, who represents agriculture as distinct from hunting or herding, and who also built the first cities and committed the first crime. According to the Genesis commentaries, Cain 'had a passion for agriculture'; and such an attachment, from the point of view of the nomadic hunter-herdsman and casual tiller of the ground, was a sharp downward step: professional agriculture means settling in one place, which leads to the construction of villages, which develop sooner or later into towns; and in the ancient world, just as the life of a shepherd was always associated with innocence, towns were always considered, relatively speaking, as places of corruption. Tacitus tells us that the Germans of his time had a horror of houses; and even today there are some nomadic or semi-nomadic peoples, like the Red Indians for example, who have a spontaneous contempt for anything which, like agriculture, would fix them in one place and thus curtail their liberty.

> The red man has no intention of 'fixing' himself on this earth where everything, according to the law of stabilization and also of condensation—'petrification' one might say—is liable to become 'crystallized'; and this explains the Indian's aversion to houses, especially stone ones, and also the absence of a writing, which according to this perspective, would 'fix' and 'kill' the sacred flow of the Spirit.[1]

1. Frithjof Schuon, *The Feathered Sun* (World Wisdom Books, Bloomington, 1990) p. 67.

This quotation brings us from the question of agriculture to that of literacy; and in this connection we may remember that the Druids also, as Caesar tells us, held that to commit their sacred doctrines to writing would be to desecrate them. Many other examples could be brought forward to show that the absence of writing, like the absence of agriculture, can have a positive cause; and in any case, however accustomed we may be to thinking of linguistic prowess as inseparable from literacy, a moment's reflection is enough to show that there is no basic connection between the two, for linguistic culture is altogether independent of the written alphabet, which comes as a very late appendix to the history of language as a whole. As Ananda Coomaraswamy pointed out with reference to what he calls 'that whole class of prophetic literature that includes the Bible, the Vedas, the Edda, the great epics, and in general the world's "best books"': 'Of these books many existed long before they were written down, many have never been written down, and others have been or will be lost.'[1]

Countless altogether illiterate men have been masters of highly elaborate languages.

'I am inclined to think that dialect the best which is spoken by the most illiterate in the islands . . . men with clear heads and wonderful memories, generally very poor and old, living in remote corners of remote islands, and speaking only Gaelic.'[2]

'The ability of oral tradition to transmit great masses of verse for hundreds of years is proved and admitted . . . .. To this oral literature, as the French call it, education is no friend. Culture destroys it, sometimes with amazing rapidity. When a nation begins to read . . . what was once the possession of the folk as a whole becomes the heritage of the illiterate only, and soon, unless it is gathered up by the antiquary, vanishes altogether.'[3]

'If we have to single out the factor which caused the decline of English village culture we should have to say it was literacy.'[4]

1. A. K. Coomaraswamy, *The Bugbear of Literacy* (Sophia Perennis, 1979), p. 25.

2. J. F. Campbell, *Popular Tales of the West Highlands* (Birlinn, 1994).

3. G. L. Kittredge in his introduction to F. G. Childe's *English and Scottish Popular Ballads* (Hippocrene Books, 1989).

4. W. G. Archer, *The Blue Grove*, preface (G. Allen & Unwin, London, 1940).

In the New Hebrides 'the children are educated by listening and watching . . . without writing, memory is perfect, tradition exact. The growing child is taught all that is known . . .. Songs are a form of storytelling . . .. The layout and content in the thousand myths which every child learns (often word perfect, and one story may last for hours) are a whole library . . . the hearers are held in a web of spun words.'

They converse together 'with that accuracy and pattern of beauty in words that we have lost . . .. The natives easily learn to write after white impact. They regard it as a curious and useless performance. They say: "Cannot a man remember and speak?"'[1]

In addition to these quotations, all of which I have taken from Coomaraswamy, it may be remarked that among the pre-Islamic Arabs it was the custom of the nobles of Mecca to send their sons to be brought up among the Bedouins of the desert because these entirely illiterate nomads were known to speak a purer Arabic than their more 'civilized' brethren of the town.

There is no doubt that, in general, 'civilization' takes the edge off man's natural alertness and vigilance, qualities which are most necessary for the preservation of language. In particular, literacy lulls men into a sense of false security by giving them the impression that their everyday speech is no longer the sole treasury in which the treasure of language is safeguarded; and once the idea of two languages, one written and one spoken, has taken root, the spoken language is doomed to degenerate relatively fast and to drag down with it, eventually, also the written language—witness the new English translation of the Bible.

In the West of today, the degeneration of the spoken language has reached a point where, although a man will take more or less trouble to set down his thoughts in writing, pride of speech is something almost unknown. It is true that one is taught to avoid certain things in speaking, but this is for purely social reasons which have nothing to do with richness of sound or any other positive quality that language may have. And yet the way a man speaks remains a far more significant factor in his life than the way he writes, for it has an

---

1. T. Harrison, *Savage Civilization* (1937), pp. 45, 344, 351, 353.

accumulative effect upon the soul which a little spasmodic penning can never have.

Needless to say, the purpose of these remarks is not to deny that the written alphabet has its uses. Language tends to degenerate in the natural course of events, even among the illiterate, and accidents such as exile or foreign domination can cause all sorts of things to be forgotten in a surprisingly short space of time. How much of the spiritual heritage of the Jews might have been lost, for example, but for written records? In any case, the manifest inspiration of some of the world's calligraphic arts suggests that when men began to record the spoken word in writing, they did so 'by order of God', and not merely 'by permission of God'. It is not, after all, writing but printing that is responsible for having turned the world into the great rubbish-heap of books that it is today. None the less, writing cannot be said to confer any superiority on man, to say the very least, and it would no doubt even be true to say that it only became necessary, as the lesser of two evils, after a certain point of human degeneration had been reached.

Speech on the other hand was always considered to be one of the glories of man. In Judaism, as also in Islam, we find the doctrine that by Divine Revelation Adam was taught the true language, that is, the language in which the sound corresponded exactly to the sense. This conception of man's primordial speech as having been the most perfectly expressive or onomatopoeic of all languages is undoubtedly beyond the reach of any philological verification. None the less philology can give us a clear idea of the general linguistic tendencies of mankind, and in doing so it teaches us nothing which in any sense weighs against the traditional report. On the contrary, every language known to us is a debased form of some more ancient language, and the further we go back in time the more powerfully impressive language becomes. It also becomes more complex, so that the oldest known languages, those which are far older than history itself, are the most subtle and elaborate in their structure, calling for greater concentration and presence of mind in the speaker than any of the later ones can claim to do. Time always tends to diminish the individual words both in form and in sonority, while grammar and syntax become more and more simplified.

It is true that although time tends to strip language of its quality, a language will always have, quantitatively speaking, the vocabulary that its people needs. A vast increase of material objects, for example, will mean a corresponding increase in the number of nouns. But whereas in modern languages the new words have to be artificially coined and added on from the outside, the most ancient known languages may be said to possess, in addition to the words in actual use, thousands of unused words which, if required, can be produced organically, as it were, in virtue of an almost unlimited capacity for word-forming which is inherent in the structure of the language. In this respect it is the modern languages which could be called 'dead' or 'moribund'; by comparison the more ancient languages, even if they be 'dead' in the sense that they are no longer used, remain in themselves like intensely vital organisms.

This does not mean that the ancient languages—and those who spoke them—were lacking in the virtue of simplicity. True simplicity, far from being incompatible with complexity, even demands a certain complexity for its full realization. A distinction must be made between complexity, which implies a definite system or order, and complication which implies disorder and even confusion. A corresponding distinction must be made between simplicity and simplification.

The truly simple man is an intense unity: he is complete and wholehearted, not divided against himself. To keep up this close-knit integration, the soul must readjust itself altogether to each new set of circumstances, which means that there must be a great flexibility in the different psychic elements: each must be prepared to fit perfectly with all the others, no matter what the mood. This closely woven synthesis, upon which the virtue of simplicity is based, is a complexity as distinct from a complication; and it has its counterpart in the complexity of the ancient languages to which the term 'synthetic' is generally applied to distinguish them from modern 'analytical' languages. It is only by an elaborate system of grammatical rules that the different parts of speech, analogous to the different elements in the soul, may be inflected so as to fit closely together, giving to each sentence something of the concentrated unity of a single word. The simplicity of the synthetic languages is in fact comparable to that of a great work of art—simplicity not necessarily of means but of total effect; and such no doubt, in an altogether superlative degree, was the simplicity of the primordial language and, we may add, of the men who spoke it. That at any rate is the conclusion to which all the available linguistic evidence points, and language is of such fundamental importance in the life of man, being so intimately bound up with the human soul of which it is the direct expression, that its testimony is of the highest psychological significance.

One of the legacies from the far past which has entered with exceptional fullness into the present, and which is therefore well qualified to serve as a 'touchstone', is the Arabic language. Its destiny has been a strange one. When the Arabs first appear in history they are a race of poets, with a wide and varied range of metrical forms, almost their only prose being their everyday speech. They possessed a somewhat rudimentary script, which only a few of them could use, but in any case they preferred to pass down their poems by living word of mouth, and until the coming of Islam they were probably the most illiterate of all Semitic peoples. No doubt this explains, at least in part, why their language was so remarkably well preserved: although linguistic evidence shows it to be a falling away from an even more archaic, that is, an even more complex and more fully sonorous language, Arabic was still, in AD 600, more archaic in form and therefore nearer to 'the language of Shem' than was the Hebrew spoken by Moses over two thousand years previously. It was Islam, or more particularly the need to record every syllable of the Koran with absolute precision, which imposed literacy on the seventh-century Arabs; but at the same time, the Koran imposed its own archaic language as a model, and since it was to be learned by heart and recited as much as possible, the detrimental effect of literacy was counteracted by the continual presence of Koranic Arabic upon men's tongues. A special science was quickly evolved for recording and preserving the exact pronunciation; and language debasement was also checked by the sustained efforts of Muslims throughout the centuries to model their speech upon the speech of their Prophet. As a result, his language is still living today. Inevitably dialects have been formed from it in the course of time through leaving out syllables, merging two different sounds into one, and other simplifications, and these dialects, which vary from one Arab country to another, are normally used in conversation. But the slightest formality of occasion calls at once for a return to the undiminished majesty and sonority of classical Arabic, which is sometimes spontaneously reverted to in conversation also, when anyone feels he has something really important to say. On the other hand, those few who on principle refuse to speak the colloquial language at all are liable to find themselves in a dilemma: either they must abstain altogether from taking part in an 'ordinary conversation' or else they must run the risk of producing an incongruous effect, like street urchins masquerading in royal robes. Idle chattering, that is, the quick expression of unweighed thoughts, must have been something comparatively unknown in the far past, for it is something that ancient languages do not lend themselves to; and if men thought less glibly, and took more trouble to compose the expression of their thoughts, they certainly took more trouble to utter them. Sanskrit tells the same story as Arabic: each, with its marvellous range and variety of consonantal sounds, leaves us no option but to conclude that in the far past man's organs of articulation and hearing were considerably finer and more delicate than they are today; and this is fully confirmed also by a study of ancient music, with all its rhythmic and melodic subtlety.[1]

If philology cannot reach the origins of language, it can none the less survey, in one unbroken sweep, thousands of years of linguistic history which means also, in a certain respect, thousands of years of the history of the human soul, a history that is one-sided, no doubt, but remarkably definite as far as it goes. In the light of this vista, which takes us far back into what is called 'prehistory', we are forced to take note of a relentless trend; and this trend is itself simply one aspect of a more general tendency which, as Dewar remarks, most physicists, chemists, mathematicians and astronomers are agreed upon, namely that 'the universe is like a clock which is running down'. So far religion and science stand together. But religion

---

1. See, for example, Alain Daniélou, *Introduction to the Study of Musical Scales* (Oriental Book Reprint Corporation, 1996).

adds—as science cannot without going beyond the scope of its function—that there is a way of escape for individuals from the collective downstream drift, and that it is possible for some to resist it, and for some even to make upstream headway against it, and for a few to overcome it altogether by making their way, in this life even, back as far as the source itself.

TWO

*

The Rhythms of Time

IT WAS easy for the ancients all over the world to believe in the sudden primordial establishment on earth of human perfection—a zenith from which there could be no rising but only falling away—because they saw that this first Divine intervention was continually repeated in lesser interventions. As regards our own forebears, the Old Testament is the story of a downward trend, as for example between the Fall and the Flood,[1] and then between the Flood and the Tower of Babel, a trend which is from time to time cut short, sometimes even by a re-establishment of relative perfection; and as soon as the grip of the Divine intervention relaxes its hold, the fatal trend reasserts itself once more, as if by a law of gravity.

It should be easier for us to see how the world goes than it was for our ancestors, for we have a wider view of history than they had, and history as a whole, in its fundamental aspects, tells the same story as that of the Old Testament and confirms its rhythm. The key events of the last three thousand years, the missions of Buddha,[2] Christ and Muhammad, were sudden interventions: they did not follow

---

1. We might say also 'between the Creation and the Fall', because this gradual deterioration is prefigured in the Earthly Paradise itself: there was a 'time' when Eve was not yet distinct from Adam, another 'time' when, although a separate being, she had not yet eaten of the forbidden fruit, and another 'time' when she, but not yet Adam, had eaten of it.

2. We will come back later to the question of the differences between one religious perspective and another. For the moment let it be admitted that although there can be no true religion without the Divine Word, we cannot presume to limit the activities of the Word either in time or in space. Moreover we have been given a criterion for judging where and where not the seeds of religious truth have been sown, for 'by their fruits ye shall know them'.

smoothly in the wake of events which preceded them; they were in opposition to the general trend of events. In each case a small nucleus of humanity was snatched up and placed on a spiritual summit to act as an ideal and a guiding light for future generations. In view of such known historical events, it is not difficult to believe that the world should have received its first spirituality also—and in this particular case its first humanity—as something in the nature of a serene thunderbolt.

This 'God-man' rhythm, a sudden rise followed by a gradual fall, the result of a combination of what is above time with what is subject to time, might be described in seasonal terms as a sudden spring racing into summer followed by a gradual autumn. How soon the autumn begins will depend on various factors. The great spring-summer of mankind as a whole, the Golden Age, is said to have lasted, according to some interpretations of the Hindu Purānas, for twenty-five thousand human years, and according to others for well over one and a half million. As regards the lesser cycles, such as those of the different religions, they are inevitably affected by their position in the great cycle. The initial spring-summer of one of the later religions, situated as it is in the autumn of the great cycle, is bound to be drawn relatively quickly towards its own autumn,[1] within which however there are the spring-summers of yet smaller cycles, for a great Saint sometimes has a mission of sudden redress which makes his appearance analogous, on a lesser scale, to that of the founder of the religion. To see this rhythm we must look at the backbone of history rather than at its surfaces, for although spirituality itself is by definition above time; the less direct effects of spirituality in time naturally tend to follow the temporal rhythm of gradual waxing and waning. It took Buddhism, Christianity and Islam some time to spread out to their full extent over those portions of humanity for which Providence would seem to have intended them: the theocratic civilizations in question, with all their sciences and arts and

1. As regards England, for example, the spring-summer of Christianity began at the end of the sixth century, and perhaps it would not be far wrong to say—though clearly no one could presume to insist on this point—that the autumn had already set in by the time of the Norman Conquest.

crafts, clearly developed more gradually than the spirituality itself, though the 'God–man' rhythm is always lying in ambush as it were, ready to rise to the surface at a moment's notice, for the more man is inspired in the true sense of the word, the more his activities will escape from the lower rhythm and the more they will conform to the higher one.

Art, for instance, in its highest aspects, is inextricably bound up with spirituality, though artistic inspiration by no means always comes at the very outset of a religion, for when spirituality in general is at its highest, men have less need of art than at any other time. In Christendom the decadent Greco-Roman style lingered on in some domains for three or four centuries before it was replaced by a genuinely Christian style; but the replacement was often more or less sudden.

To take a supreme example of art, the Jews had had no sacred architecture until Solomon built the Temple according to the plans which had been revealed to David. So sudden was the attainment of this architectural zenith that the builders had to be brought in from outside. Though this example is exceptional, being something more even than inspiration, namely direct revelation, inspiration none the less moves in a similar way. The earliest art that has come down to us is a striking example—sufficiently striking to force itself even upon those whose ideas it completely contradicts and who are 'perplexed' by what would in fact be perplexing if it were otherwise.

'Undoubtedly the most perplexing aspect of the art phenomenon when it appears to us for the first time is the high degree of maturity shown in the earliest expressions. The sudden appearance of stylistically evolved works of art takes us completely by surprise, with a marvellous eruption of aesthetic values . . . even the examples which belong unquestionably to the earliest phase . . . are works of amazing artistic maturity.'[1]

Many things are inexplicable unless we realize that there are two 'currents' or 'rhythms' at work in history instead of only one. Our ancestors were without any doubt aware of both, for everyone

1. Paolo Graziosi, *Palaeolithic Art* (Faber & Faber, 1960), pp. 23–24.

knows the surface current of gradual waxing and waning, and as to the sudden 'up' and gradual 'down' which are inevitable as regards all that is most qualitative in a civilization, did not Christians always look back to the early fathers with especial reverence[1] and above all, beyond these, to the Apostles themselves?

Similarly in Islam, whatever may have been achieved in lesser domains by later generations, Muslims have never had any difficulty —to say the least—in assenting with wholehearted conviction to the saying of their Prophet:

'The best of my people are my generation; then they that come immediately after them; then they that come immediately after those.'

To take yet another example: 'According to Buddhists there are three periods during which our capacity for understanding Buddhism grows less and less. These are counted from the death of Buddha: the first, which lasts for a thousand years, is called "the period of true Buddhism"; the second, also of a thousand years, is called "the period of imitation Buddhism"; the third, in which we are, we the men of the "Last Days", is the period of degeneration.'[2]

The adherents of these three religions are not exceptional in their point of view. In fact, it would be true to say of all civilizations that history has record of, except the modern one, that they were pervaded by a general consciousness of imperfection, of falling far short of an ideal; and that ideal, which was kept fresh in men's intelligences by a chain of Saints across the centuries, had had its greatest profusion of flowering among the first representatives of the religion in question. Behind this summit, beyond the flats of intervening decadence—for of previous civilizations it was mostly no more than the decadent tail-ends that were known—there loomed the summit of the perfection of Primordial Man.

---

1. St Benedict spoke in advance with the voice of the whole of the Middle Ages when he said: 'The conferences of the fathers and their institutes and their lives . . . what else are they but store-houses of the virtues of good-living and obedient monks? But to us, indolent, ill-living and negligent, belong shame and confusion' (*The Rule of Saint Benedict*, SPCK), p. 106.

2. Kanei Okamoto, Jodo bonze, quoted by E. Steinilder-Oberlin. *Les Sectes bouddhiques Japonaises* (G. Crès & Cie, Paris, 1930), p. 200.

According to the Jewish tradition, if Adam did not at first possess 'the knowledge of good and evil', he surpassed even the angels in his knowledge of God; and although if we move to the Far East the manner of expression becomes very different, the truth that is expressed remains the same. Over two thousand years ago in China the Taoist sage Chuang Tzu said:

'The knowledge of the ancients was perfect. How perfect? At first they did not yet know that there were things (apart from *Tao*, the Way, which signifies the Eternal and Infinite). This is the most perfect knowledge; nothing can be added. Next, they knew that there were things, but did not yet make distinctions between them. Next they made distinctions between them but they did not yet pass judgements upon them. When judgements were passed, [the knowledge of] *Tao* was destroyed.'[1]

Very different again outwardly, and yet essentially the same, is the message of an old Lithuanian song which has come down to us out of the shadows of prehistory. This song tells us how 'the Moon married the Sun in the first spring', and then how the Moon 'straying alone' caught sight of the Morning Star and fell in love with it, whereupon God, the Father of the Sun, cut the Moon in two.

The sun is universally the symbol of the Spirit, and sunlight symbolizes direct knowledge of spiritual truths, whereas the moon represents all that is human and in particular the mind, mental knowledge being, like moonlight, indirect and reflected. It is through the mind that 'distinctions are made' and 'judgements are passed'.

'The Moon married to the Sun' is Primordial Man with his two natures, human and Divine; and just as the moon reflects the sun, so the human soul in all its faculties and virtues reflects the Divine Qualities. Thus the moon as a symbol of the human nature expresses the universal doctrine that man is 'made in the image of God', and that he is 'the representative of God on earth'.

Creation means separation from God. The act of creating set in motion an outward, separative tendency to which all creatures as such are subject. But in the non-human creatures this tendency is arrested by lack of freedom. Being no more than remote and frag-

1. Yu-Lan-Fung's translation, p. 53.

mentary reflections of the Creator they only reflect His Free Will in a very limited sense; and if they have less freedom than man for good, they have also less freedom to degenerate. For man the outward urge born of creation was perfectly balanced 'in the first spring' by the inward magnetism of his higher nature.

The meeting point of the two natures, the summit of the soul which is also its centre—for the Kingdom of Heaven is 'within' as well as 'above'—is what most religions name the Heart (written here throughout with a capital to distinguish it from the centre of the body); and the Heart is the throne of the Intellect in the sense in which *Intellectus* was used throughout the Middle Ages, that is, the 'solar' faculty which perceives spiritual truths directly unlike the 'lunar' faculties of reason, memory and imagination, which are the differentiated reflections of the Intellect.

In virtue of 'the marriage of the Moon and the Sun' the out-branching, separative 'knowledge of good and evil' was completely subordinated to the inward-pointing, unitive Heart-knowledge which refers all creatures back to their Creator. 'The cutting of the Moon in two' denotes the separation of Heart and mind, of Intellect and reason, and man's consequent loss of direct, unitive knowledge and his subjection to the dualism of indirect knowledge, the knowledge of good and evil.

It was mental independence, represented by 'the Moon straying alone', which brought with it the possibility of purely profane impulses and actions. There was nothing spiritual in the Moon's forsaking the greater light for the lesser, just as there was nothing spiritual in the impulse which caused Pandora to open her box, or in that which caused the eating of the forbidden fruit; and the significance of this last act may be further understood in the light of the Zoroastrian religion according to which one stage in the corruption of man is marked by the enjoyment of food for its own sake and the failure to attribute its goodness to the Creator.

The Edenic state was in a sense above time, for there were no seasons and no death. Nor was there any religion, for the end to which religion is a means had not yet been lost, whereas the Golden Age, which begins immediately after the Fall, is by definition the age of religion, being named in Sanskrit *Krita-Yuga* because in it all men 'performed perfectly' their religious duties. According to Hinduism the normal span of mortal life was then a thousand years, and this seems to be confirmed by Judaism. It is understandable however that Judaism and other still later religions do not dwell on the excellence of that age, for however good it may have been in itself; it none the less contained the seeds of ruin and had already been brought as it were into discredit by the Iron Age, the ultimate fruit of those seeds.

For the earlier religions the Golden Age stood for the supreme ideal of what was possible in earthly conditions after the Fall. But the nearer the cycle drew to its end, the more out of reach that ideal became. None the less, if we look at the extremely elliptical first chapters of Genesis, the Golden Age is there, not explicitly but in undeniable implication, personified by Adam after the Fall; and when we turn to the Genesis commentaries and to the Jewish apocryphal books we find Adam extolled not merely as being unique among men for having committed one sin only, but also as a great visionary: he is the Prophet who inaugurated religion upon earth; and at his death the Archangels descended from Heaven to bury him. We read moreover that in the times of Adam and Seth the corpses of the dead did not putrefy, and men were still born 'in the image of God',[1] whereas after Seth this was no longer the case, and the mountains, which had hitherto been fertile, became barren rock.

*

1. See *Midrash Rabbah* on Genesis IV, 26 (Soncino Press, London, 1939), vol. 1, p. 196. In one sense—for a sacred text has always been held to be a synthesis of different meanings at different levels—the story of Adam, Cain and Abel comprises the whole history of mankind: today the transgression of Cain is almost complete, the nomads having been almost altogether put out of existence by the town dwellers (see René Guénon, *The Reign of Quantity and the Signs of the Times*, Ch. 21, Sophia Perennis, Ghent, NY, 1995). From this point of view it may be said that a new allegory begins with the Adam-Seth narrative. But from another point of view, if Cain as it were recapitulates the fall and personifies all the 'worldly wisdom' which resulted from it, and if Abel stands for the loss of Eden, personifying the repentance of Adam and his expiation, Seth represents the relenting of God towards Adam and the establishment of the Golden Age.

According to the Hindus, during the cycle of the four ages the downward trend is interrupted by eight sudden redresses, each brought about by the incarnation on earth of an aspect of the Divinity. The cycle is also inaugurated and closed by similar incarnations or 'descents' *(Avataras)* as they are called, which brings the number up to ten. The ninth was the Buddha who is called the *Mleccha Avatara* (the Foreign Descent), for although he appeared as a Hindu, the destined scope of his mission lay outside the frontiers of Hinduism. The Brahmanic perspective could hardly fail to include this Divine intervention, though being naturally more or less limited to what concerns Hindus, it does not take into consideration the religions of the West; but the tenth descent, which has yet to take place, is for the whole world.

Kalki, the name of this last and tenth *Avatara*, is represented as riding on a white horse, sword in hand, and some descriptions of him bear a marked resemblance to verses in the Apocalypse. The *Kalki Avatara* is expected to put an end to the Dark Age, and to inaugurate a new cycle with a Golden Age.

This expectation, which all religions share, whatever name they may give to Kalki, has nothing in common with the modern belief in 'progress'. It is true that some of our contemporaries prefer to believe that it was human progress which eventually earned the first coming of Christ, and that still further progress will finally make the world fit for his second coming. But such ideas are altogether alien to mediaeval and ancient concepts. Far from holding that mankind had earned the Redemption, our ancestors believed that it was a pure Grace; and as to Christ's second coming, they believed that the signs of its imminence would be, not the virtues of an almost perfect world waiting for a final perfecting touch, but 'wars', 'rumours of wars', 'earthquakes', 'famines', and civil discords with 'brother against brother', 'father against son', 'children against parents' and finally 'the abomination of desolation'. According to the sayings of Christ and the Prophets, which for our ancestors were fully confirmed by the rhythm of history, the Millennium was not something which would be led up to, but something which would be led down to, at least in so far as concerns the human collectivity taken as a whole. It was believed that a gradual decline, interrupted by certain redresses,[1] would lead to 'great tribulation such as was not since the beginning of the world',[2] and one may compare Christ's description of the signs which would mark the approach of his second coming with what other religions teach about the same event. The lowest ebb of humanity was to be marked by the reign of the Antichrist. Then the true Christ would appear, as suddenly 'as the lightning cometh out of the East and shineth even unto the West'.[3]

*

The question as to whether knowledge of modern discoveries would have changed the ancients' belief in the excellence of their ancestors has already been asked, and in part answered. But what of their expectations for the future? If long dead generations could return to earth, would they feel that they and their Prophets had been mistaken? Or would a sight of the modern world confirm their gloomiest forebodings about the future of mankind? This question also has already been answered implicitly; the next chapters are more explicit.

1. Is there anything in ancient belief from which we might conclude the probability or even the possibility of a redress between now and the end of the cycle? A part answer to this question may lie in the fact that when Christ said, in speaking of the signs which would precede his second coming 'And except those days should be shortened, there should be no flesh saved; but for the elect's sake those days shall be shortened' (St Matthew, xxiv, 22), he was clearly not referring to the final 'passing away' of 'the first heaven and the first earth' in preparation for a 'new heaven and a new earth' but to a preliminary partial destruction. The 'days' in question would seem to be none other than what the Red Indians, in particular the Hopis, call Purification Day, which they consider to be imminent. As the word 'purification' suggests, they expect the destruction to have also a positive aspect. Islam likewise has always looked forward to a short-lived spiritual regeneration with the coming of the Mahdi, in the years immediately preceding the Antichrist; and in Christ's prophecy, the reason why the days of destruction are to be shortened suggests that they will be followed by a kind of spiritual redress, if only a fleeting and a fragmentary one.

2. St Matthew, xxiv, 21.

3. Ibid, 27.

THREE

The Present in the Light of the Past

IN THE PAST, long before our times, there were isolated instances of attempts to invent a means of raising the body into the air, in imitation of the flight of birds, but only today, as far as we know, has any real success been achieved in this respect, and it is only today that there has developed a general interest in such exploits. The enormous and widespread enthusiasm for the 'conquest of space' and for eventual 'voyages to Mars' cannot be altogether separated from the ascent of Everest and other feats of climbing. In all these activities no doubt one of the motives is idle curiosity, the heritage of Pandora. But strange though it may seem, in addition to this outward-pointing and disintegrative tendency which may be said to have caused the Fall, is there not also at work the subconscious motive of regaining what was lost by the Fall?

The distinctive feature of Primordial Man was that he had a superhuman as well as a human nature; and man still retains virtually in the depths of his being the need to transcend his humanity, to move 'upstream' against the current, and to re-establish the connection between the soul which is human and the Heart which is Divine. In an age when, generally speaking, this need is utterly frustrated on the plane of the soul where alone it has meaning, the ineradicable urge to go beyond the normal sphere of humanity is forced to manifest itself on a lower plane. Hence what might be called the superstition of 'up and beyond', for a superstition is something which is 'left over' from the past and which continues to prevail without being understood.

In all religions there is a doctrine of three worlds, the worlds of the Spirit, the soul and the body. The soul and the body, the psychic and the corporeal, together make up what is commonly called 'this world'. The world of the Spirit, whose gateway is the Heart, altogether transcends this world, being beyond the reach of any human faculty. The superhuman faculty which is enthroned in the Heart and which is the means of connection between the soul and the Spirit is, as we have seen, what our ancestors called the Intellect.

In Hinduism this faculty of transcendent vision is represented in statues and other forms of sacred art by a third eye placed in the middle of the forehead. In Christianity and Islam it is named the 'Eye of the Heart' which in Arabic, the sacred language of Islam, means also 'the Fountain of the Heart', and it is at this fountain that the soul drinks the 'Elixir of Life'. In Christianity also the two symbolisms are combined, for there is a tradition that when Lucifer fell from Heaven his frontal eye dropped to earth in the form of an emerald, which was then carved into the cup of the Holy Grail.

Thought, which includes the reason, imagination and memory, is in itself a purely human faculty, but through the virtual continuity which exists between the soul and the Spirit, thought may be penetrated in a certain measure by the light of the Intellect. The purpose of metaphysics, the study of what is 'beyond nature' that is, beyond this world, is to open the mind to this penetration and to give the thoughts an upward bent. This is, strictly speaking, the greatest elevation that man as such is capable of, for beyond this the human ends and the superhuman begins. None the less, the essential characteristic of man is his contact with the superhuman, and this paradox is expressed in the Taoist term *Chenn-jen* (True Man) which is only applied to a man whose soul has regained contact with the Spirit.

Western thought has been increasingly dominated for the last four hundred years by humanism, which is centred not on the concept of 'True Man' but on 'man as we know him to be', that is, the highest member of the animal kingdom. It is ironical that by failing to be interested in the superhuman, or by casting doubts upon its existence, humanism which purports to be the glorification of man, should seek to deprive the human mind of all its truly upward possibilities, confining it as it were to a low-roofed building where it can scarcely stand upright, let alone fly.

Modern philosophy is frankly uninterested in the higher reaches of the universe; and in general it would be more to the point if such words as intellect and metaphysics were stored away as relics of the past, like crown jewels in a state which has changed from a kingdom to a republic. But such scrupulousness would be too unflattering and too much of a betrayal. There would be no glamour in describing some hero of modern science or letters as 'a very cerebral person'; and so it comes about that a man may spend a large part of his life in altogether anti-intellectual activities, and even in maintaining that there exists nothing higher than the human soul and yet he may be currently referred to as 'one of the leading intellectuals of our day'. Not that the word has really changed its meaning, for we are still too near in time to Meister Eckhardt's formulation:

'There is something in the soul which is uncreated . . .. This is the Intellect.'

There is still a difference between calling a man 'brainy' and calling him intellectual, for this last word retains a suggestion of something mysteriously exalted—hence its value for purposes of pretension. Similarly, when a dictator of the former Soviet Union spoke of the 'material and spiritual benefits of Communism', he preferred to utter a contradiction in terms (for a Communist, by definition, does not believe in the Spirit) than submit to the inglorious banality of expressing what he really meant; and further West, humanists, whether atheists or agnostics, are just as unwilling to give up the word 'spiritual', which still plays an important part in their rhetoric. Nor is there any lack today of artists and art critics who, when a work of art is nebulously devoid of meaning, will unhesitatingly describe it as 'mystical'. Yet if it be reality that is wanted—and realism is supposed to be one of the 'ideals' of our times—then let it be admitted that the space-rockets rise from a world which is in fact starved of upward movement upon all higher planes, a world dominated by an outlook which is in many respects abysmal and at the best utterly flat.

On the other hand, it would be no misuse of words to say that the outlook of the ancients was winged, since throughout their world, in the West as well as in the East, the contemplative life was generally recognized as the highest kind of life that man can lead, and its essential feature is the fixing of one's thoughts upon the Spirit in the aspiration to rise up towards it upon the wings of intellectual intuition.

The sphere of the moon is, according to ancient belief, no more than the symbol, that is, the projected shadow in the material world of time and space, of the Heaven of the Moon, the lowest of the seven Heavens and the first of the spiritual stages through which the being must pass on its journey to the Infinite and the Eternal after it has passed beyond the limits of this world. It is in the Moon that the first canto of Dante's *Paradiso* is set, for it is to this Heaven that he has risen from the Earthly Paradise after having ascended the Mountain of Purgatory. The idea of attempting to fly through space to the material moon was reserved for an age when the journey described by Dante is seldom thought of as having actually taken place.

To all this it may be objected that Dante's journey still remains in fact as real a possibility as ever, that there are some true mystics[1] alive in the modern world, and that even in the Middle Ages they were never more than a small minority. As regards this last point, the same can be said of times and places which were far better than mediaeval Europe. The Iron Age as a whole takes another of its names, the Dark Age, from the fact that the mystics, who are the light of the earth, are in a minority. None the less, even so late on in the Iron Age as the time of Dante, that minority, far from being pushed to one side, was fully in line with the majority, for it represented men's highest ideals. Europe was still under the spell of Christ and therefore of the Gospel story of Mary and Martha: as the heirs of Mary and the possessors of 'the one thing needful', that minority stood as it were at the top of a pyramid, marking a norm towards which a self-confessedly abnormal majority looked up, and from

---

1. The word 'mystical' partly coincides with 'intellectual', for a mystic is one who perceives, or who aspires to perceive, the mysteries of the Kingdom of Heaven, and the Intellect is the faculty through which this perception takes place. On the whole, 'mystical' tends to be the more general word and 'intellectual' refers rather to the mystic path of knowledge than to that of love, though here again 'intellectual love' is sometimes used in the sense of 'mystic love' or 'spiritual love'. For a clear and far-reaching definition of these two mystic paths, see Frithjof Schuon, *Gnosis* (Sophia Perennis, 1990), pp. 38–39.

which a spiritual influence could flow down throughout the different strata of society. In a sense that pyramid still exists, because its existence is in the very nature of things; but 'officially' it has been razed to the ground.

*

According to the Hindu Purānas, bodily sickness was unknown until well on into the Dwāpara Yuga, that is, the Bronze Age, the third of the four. As to the ancient sciences of healing which have been handed down from prehistoric times among various peoples, the function of the 'medicine man' is very often simply part of the function of the priest, and in any case the science itself is always intimately bound up with religion. For this reason it is also more or less connected with the other ancient sciences, each of which was itself an offshoot of religion, being based on the knowledge of certain cosmological truths which according to tradition first came to man through inspiration and in some cases through revelation.

These truths are all aspects of the harmony of the universe: they are the correspondences between the microcosm, the macrocosm and the metacosm, that is, between the little world of the human individual, the big outside world, and the next world which transcends both. To take one example, each of the planets (that is, those planets which are visible to the naked eye, together with the sun, making seven in all) corresponds to a particular metal, to certain stones, plants and animals, to a particular colour, and to a note in the musical scale; it has its day of the week, and its hours of every day; it presides over certain parts of the body; it corresponds to certain sicknesses, and on the psychic plane to certain temperaments, virtues and vices, and metaphysically to one of the Seven Heavens and to certain Angelic Powers, Saints, Prophets and Divine Names.

One science could never come near to embracing all the secrets of the universe, and consequently there are many different traditional sciences of medicine; but generally speaking, the expert practice of one of these presupposed some understanding not merely of physiology, biology, botany, mineralogy, chemistry and physics (approached from an angle altogether different from that of the modern sciences), but also of astrology and sometimes of music, as well as of what are sometimes called the sciences of numbers and letters, to which must be added metaphysics and theology, including a wide practical knowledge of liturgy, all combined with an outstanding natural aptitude for healing.

While allowing for frequent exaggerations, it would be foolish to disbelieve all that tradition has handed down in widely different parts of the world about remarkable cures effected by ancient sciences. But between them and modern medicine there is no bridge. A branch of the ancient Chinese science of medicine, known to the West as 'acupuncture', which is still widely practised in China and Japan, has been adopted in a somewhat fragmentary way by an increasing number of Western doctors who have been won over by its remarkable efficacity. But it is doubtful whether it could ever become generally acceptable to the modern medical world, for it is based on very unobvious relations between widely different parts of the body, correspondences which no mere experimental investigations could ever have detected and which modern science cannot account for.

Some of those Western doctors who practise acupuncture do in fact try to bring it into line with modern medicine by maintaining that it must have originated through experiments; but this is a pure hypothesis, and apart from the undeniable fact that the ancient approach to science, the world over, was radically different from the modern one, is it really conceivable that it could have been discovered as a result of experiments that for a complaint of the stomach, for example, treatment may be applied to a nerve centre in the toe, whereas the liver can be treated through the ankle, the kidney through the knee, the great intestine through the elbow, and so on?[1]

Apart from a few exceptional and often superficial intrusions of such sciences into the modern one, and allowing for some continuity between past and present (perhaps more than one is aware of as regards the use of drugs), modern medicine is what it claims to be, a purely human invention based on man's own unaided practical experiments.

1. For a study of this science as practised in the West, see Felix Mann, *Acupuncture*, Butterworth-Heineman, 1992.

The vocation of a doctor still has, unquestionably, the sacredness which belongs to every response to an urgent need; and it might be argued that this applies also to his science, despite its intrinsic non-sacred character, for although most modern inventions have not 'necessity' for their 'mother', a few have, especially medical ones. If a man could come from the far past into the present, which would strike him most, the skill of our dentists, for example, or the rottenness of our teeth? It might even be said that in a grossly over-populated disease ridden world, where ill health is on the increase almost as much as the gifts to practice a sacred science are on the decrease, there is need in particular for the modern science of medicine, that is, a science which is not too exacting as regards qualifications and can be taught to large numbers of men and women who can be drilled and organized to meet the crisis.

It is extremely doubtful, however, whether our ancestors would have admitted all this. In any case they would certainly have maintained that the humanistic point of view which had made the development of modern medicine possible had itself provoked many of the ills which call for medical treatment. Nor would it have escaped their notice that like humanism in general, this particular manifestation of humanism—and the same applies to other modern sciences—has a suicidal aspect to it. For just as humanism means the abolition of humanity, that is, the elimination of all the specific characteristics of what the Taoists call True Man, modern medicine means, in the long run, the abolition of health through degeneration of the species caused by the development of a system which allows man, and therefore in a sense forces him, to flout on an enormous scale the law of natural selection which is nature's antidote to decadence. To say that we live in a world where everybody is half dead because nobody dies is clearly an exaggeration, but that at least is the trend; and in ultimately defeating its own ends this science is doomed to be one of the modern world's many illustrations of the truth of the parable of the talents according to which, 'From him that hath not shall be taken away even that which he hath'.

But if medical science has now escaped from man's control in more senses than one, by far the most sinister aspect to the situation is that it has taken on its present pseudo-absolute importance by usurping in a very large measure the place of something which does in fact touch upon the Absolute. The modern world devotes to the treatment of sick bodies an incalculable store of energy which in the past was devoted to the treatment of sick souls. Men were brought up in the consciousness that all souls are sick, save only the rarest exceptions. Modern standards also, needless to say, allow that many souls are sick, and we are continually being warned that both criminals and madmen are on the increase. But the vast majority of souls, those of the law-abiding and the sane, are now considered to be in good health or at any rate well enough to require practically no treatment, and it is assumed that they are more or less immune from deterioration. The gulf which separates this so-called 'good health' from perfect health is lost sight of; and in general ideas as to what perfect health of soul might be are very vague; nor on the whole do they seem to have been much less vague in recent generations, those of the last two or three centuries, whose increasingly unintelligent and often perfunctory moralism was bound to provoke in the end a reaction of amoral scepticism.

On the other hand, if our less recent ancestors knew so well that their souls were sick, and if they understood so well the nature of the sickness, it was because their civilization was founded on the idea of psychic health and dominated by the concept of the perfect soul. Nor were they alone, for this concept, being based on universal principles, cannot truly be said to have varied from one end of the ancient world to the other, except where religion had degenerated to the point of losing sight of the very purpose of its existence, which is above all to reunite man with his Absolute, Eternal and Infinite Source. Wherever religion keeps this end in view, the conception of the highest human possibility necessarily remains the same; and always allowing for certain differences of formulation, the great religions of the world are in fact unanimous that the essential feature of one who, having regained the state of Primordial Man, has thereby regained full health of soul, is an awareness of 'the Kingdom of Heaven within him': he has no need to 'seek' for he has already 'found', no need to 'knock' for it has already been 'opened unto him'; and through this opening the mirror-like human soul is able to reflect the Divine Qualities and to be, as it was created, 'in the image of God'.

The Qualities are represented in Islamic doctrine as being of two kinds, Qualities of Majesty and Qualities of Beauty, and this accords with what other religions teach, implicitly if not expressly, about the Divine Perfection.[1] The highest ideal on the human plane may therefore be defined as majesty and beauty of soul, to which must be added, in the very nature of things, holiness and humility,[2]—holiness in virtue of the soul's direct contact with the Spirit, and humility because only the soul which has access to the Spirit is fully conscious, by comparison, of the limitations of the soul as such.

For every theocratic civilization this ideal is incarnate above all in the Divine Messenger, the founder of the religion on which the civilization is based, and in the nucleus of men and women who were his companions and immediate successors. It is enshrined in their tombs, as also in those of later Saints, and every such shrine enriches the community with yet another possibility of pilgrimage. It is glorified in the liturgy, and in poetry, painting and sculpture. Translated into the language of geometrical symbols, it stands crystallized in the majesty and beauty of the great temples where it is also to be heard, transposed into the medium of rhythm and cadence; and this music, flowing out into the world, sets its seal more or less deeply on all non-liturgical music of all classes of society, just as the dwellings of both rich and poor are prolongations, in various ways and in varying degrees, of the central, communal place of worship.

Holiness and humility are represented by the head and the foot of the Cross; majesty, including justice and other virtues which reflect the Divine Rigour, is represented by the left arm, and beauty, including all reflections of the Divine Mercy, by the right. In a higher sense, majesty is a reflection of the Absolute and the Eternal; as such, inseparable from holiness, and including implicitly all virtue, it is symbolized by the vertical of the Cross, while beauty, including explicitly all the virtues and reflecting the Infinite Riches and Bounty of God, is figured in the amplitude of the horizontal.

1. In the Far Eastern tradition these two aspects of Divinity are symbolized respectively by the dragon and the phoenix, in the Greco-Roman tradition by the eagle and the peacock.

2. In Christianity these two virtues, as also majesty and beauty, are reflected in the double name *Jesu-Maria*.

Through the converging of its extremities into its centre the Cross is also a figure of unity, just as by pointing in all directions it is a figure of totality, and here lies another aspect of being in the image of God, who is both One and All. To be perfectly well, the soul must be complete. 'Holiness', 'wholeness' and 'health' are in origin the same word and have merely been differentiated in form and in meaning through the fragmentation of language. The virtues of sincerity and simplicity are inseparable from this perfection, for each in its own way means undividedness of soul.

The basic cause of man's sickness is the loss of the direct connection, within him, between this world and the next, and the loss, in consequence, of the soul's sensitivity to the Divine magnetism of the Heart which alone can counterbalance the out-pointing urge to which all creation is subject; and with this urge unchecked, just as the radii of a circle move further and further apart from each other the further they are prolonged from the centre, so the different psychic elements become more and more loosely knit and the soul becomes less and less of a unity, less and less simple and sincere. The wording of Christ's first commandment comes as a fulminating antidote to this chronic disintegration. The purpose of religion as a whole is to knit together all looseness in man by setting up in his soul an impetus towards the centre which will bring it once more within range of the attraction of the Heart; and if this applies above all to religious rites, it is true of everything that has a spiritual function. For example, when we contemplate a work of truly sacred art, the whole soul comes together as if in answer to an imperative summons. There is no question of any fragmentary reaction, for we cannot marvel enough. Here lies the essence of a sacred civilization, to be forever demanding, in all sorts of ways, that the soul should pull itself together and keep itself together, and in the response of souls to this demand lies one of the great superiorities of the past over the present. To take a very small, yet none the less significant example, when we listen to dance music even as late as that of the sixteenth century, and even to that of the gayer dances, we do not have in any sense the impression that a fragment of the soul has splintered off rebelliously from the rest. On the contrary such music conjures up the presence of men and women who in their pleasures could not forget, and did not desire to forget, the fleeting brevity of life and the certainty of death.

Our present civilization makes no such demands upon the soul: whatever sacramental 'medicines' a few may take, the modern world sees to it that men are perpetually surrounded by antidotes to those medicines, by all sorts of poisons that pander to the sickness instead of keeping it in check, for it is a monstrously ironical fact that the only civilization which professes to discount 'heredity' and to put all its faith in 'environment' is unique in having no positive environment to offer. It would even be no exaggeration to say that much if not most of the good that men inherit today is in serious danger of being blighted precisely by the environment they are condemned to grow up in and live out their lives in. Their education, the work that most of them have to do,[1] the clothes they have to wear,[2] and above all, perhaps, the way they are supposed to pass their leisure hours and 'enjoy themselves', are calculated not only to stifle all sense of majesty and beauty, but to eliminate the virtues of unity, simplicity

---

1. If the past could witness the present, it would cry out, with reference to most means of livelihood in the modern world: 'Was man created for this?'

2. After the body, clothes are the next nearest environment of the human soul and have an incalculable effect upon it, as the ancients well knew. Their dress, while it varied superbly from civilization to civilization, was always a reminder of the dignity of man as the representative of God on earth. But in western Europe we have to go back almost a thousand years in order to find clothes which bear comparison with those of other theocratic civilizations, or with the dignity of simple nakedness. It is true that in the late Middle Ages Christians still continued to show a certain sense of form and proportion in what they wore, but an unmistakably mundane, secular note had been struck, the fateful herald of what was to come. From the middle of the sixteenth century onwards, while the rest of the world continued to remain faithful to traditional dress, European fashions went through paroxysm after paroxysm of extravagance and vanity, a sort of death agony of spiritual values, to end up with a dress which, as the Arab says of it, 'reeks of atheism'. To have an objective view of the anti-spiritual nature of modern fashions, it is enough to remember that in the sacred art of many civilizations blessed Spirits in Paradise are pictorially represented, without the least incongruity, in clothes such as were worn by the artist and his contemporaries. Let us imagine such a picture printed by a modern artist with the figures dressed accordingly. It is significant also that the more 'correctly' they were dressed, that is, the more obtrusively representative their clothes were of today or of the last two centuries in any of their decades, the more shattering would be the effect.

and sincerity by breaking up the psychic substance into fragments. Instead of being disciplined to be always 'all there', the soul forgets how to give its whole self to anything, for there is little or nothing in its daily diet that it can come anywhere near to wholly approving of. Its environment is like a multitude of hands pulling at it from all directions as much as to say 'Give me just a small piece of your attention,' and these 'hands' are ever on the increase, and ever more trivial in their demands.

In other words, as regards psychic health, the modern world is becoming more and more like a large hospital in which ailments stand a serious risk of receiving the exact opposite of the treatment they require, a hospital as it were in which diabetics are kept on a diet of sugar—to such an extent have healers 'washed their hands' of souls, at any rate as far as concerns the law-abiding and the sane.

*

Among the correspondences on which sacred sciences are based is the correspondence between the heart as centre of the body and the sun as centre of the material world, both heart and sun being symbols of that Heart which is the Centre of all things. This knowledge of the centrality of the sun and of its symbolism is scarcely separable from the knowledge that the earth and the planets move round the sun, and it is therefore not surprising that some of the sages of antiquity should have known, in this respect, what the modern astronomer knows. But there can be little doubt that until the time of Copernicus, most men believed that the sun moved round the earth. Since his time, and above all since the time of Galileo, more and more people have come to know that it is the earth which moves round the sun; and it seems that here also they have paid for a piece of knowledge on a low plane by the loss of far more precious knowledge analogous to it on a higher plane. If the ancients in general did not know that the earth moves round the sun, they did know that the individual soul, which corresponds to the earth, moves round the inward Sun, despite the illusion that the human ego is itself an independent centre, an illusion to which fallen man by definition is in some degree subject. Today, when the human ego is, collectively speaking, near to reaching its utmost extreme of separation from the Heart, and when the veils between Heart and soul are at their thickest, the illusion of the ego's own centrality is necessarily at its strongest; and in fact most of those who acclaim Copernicus' 'discovery' as 'one of the milestones along the path of human enlightenment' are in grave doubts, when not in definite disbelief, about the very existence of the inward Sun. Not that the gaining of the lower knowledge has directly entailed the loss of the higher, though the connection between the two may be closer than it appears to be. But the loss of the one, with the gaining of the other, is undeniably a consequence of the general shift of man's 'expertness' from the spiritual to the material.

*

Flight, curing the sick, and knowledge of what is central and what peripheral are three examples of possibilities which, stifled or stunted upon a higher plane; have burst forth in riotous excrescence upon a lower plane. Let us now take a fourth example which, from its own particular angle, like each of the others, embraces the whole question.

The soul is of this world, whereas the Spirit is not; but since there was at first a relative continuity between soul and Spirit, there is a certain part of the psychic substance—that which lies at the soul's uppermost boundary nearest the Heart—which is in one sense 'not of this world' since its function is to receive from the Intellect the light of the Spirit. In another sense it is 'of this world' because its function is to transmit that light to the other faculties of the soul and also because, with the veiling of the Intellect and the sealing of the boundary between the two worlds, it was left on the soul's side of the barrier.

This highest and most precious part of the psychic substance is none other than the domain of the three virtues faith, hope and love, which are three different modes of the soul's aspiration towards the next world. Let us consider for the moment the midmost of the three, which partakes in a sense of both the others.

The virtue of hope consists in looking upon human life as a journey which leads to the infinite and eternal satisfaction of all possible desires, provided that certain conditions, well within our capabilities, are fulfilled. This end can be reached not only after death but also, by an exceptional few—exceptional, that is, at the present stage of the cycle—even during this life. In either case, in order that life may be a journey in the right direction, the conditions to be fulfilled have always to do with moving 'upstream' against the current, though there are many different ways of doing this, and some are easier for one group of humanity, some for another—hence the diversity of religions.

Within each religion too there is always a certain range of possibilities to allow for the wide differences between individuals. A life of perpetual pilgrimage, for example, is clearly very different on the surface from a life of chanting a sacred text or invoking a Divine Name in perpetual seclusion from the world; and there is also the possibility of a life which is penetrated by invocation or meditation or both but which outwardly follows a course of earning one's livelihood, and such a life may or may not be interrupted from time to time by a pilgrimage or a spiritual retreat. But whatever the outward differences, the end in view is always, ultimately, the same, the transcending of the human individuality, through a Grace called down by worship, in order to regain the lost contact with the Spirit. Even religious aspiration at its lowest, that is, a legal minimum of worship performed in fear of damnation, may be said to have this end in view, at any rate in an indirect sense, for salvation leads to purification which is itself the key to sanctification.

Such until very recently was the orientation of man all over the world: the 'boats' were all, as it were, at least pointing upstream, whether the force of the current was in fact carrying them downstream or not. But a time came, within the last two hundred years or less—it would be difficult to fix it more exactly—when for want of the minimum effort required to keep the prows in the right direction, a number of boats that had been drifting downstream backwards were deflected to meet the current broadside on and thus to be as it were with no orientation at all; and from this untenable position of doubt, uncertainty and hopelessness it was not difficult for the current to turn them right round to face the way they were drifting. With shouts of triumph that they were 'at last making some headway', they called on those who were still struggling upstream to 'throw off the fetters of superstition' and to 'move with the times'. A new creed was quickly invented, and though its implications have seldom been looked full in the face they are, clearly enough, that all man's past millennial upstream efforts, that is, 'reactionary' or 'retrograde' efforts, were completely wasted, having been utterly pointless and misguided; but 'in spite of all that reactionaries could do to keep mankind in the dark night of ignorance, the progressive element in humanity has gradually been fighting its way forward', so that we have now arrived at what was described by a politician in the twenties of the last century as 'the glorious morning of the world'.

Meantime their 'doctrine' is made all the more plausible by the annexation of most of the eminent men of the past as having been in direct line with themselves. Not only are the revolutionaries acclaimed as having been the champions of progress in their day, but also the great spiritual figures. With a blind eye turned to the fact that their mission was to lead men back to the primordial perfection in which mankind was created, Buddha, Christ and Muhammad are pronounced to have been 'far ahead of their times'.

In fact, the saying 'man cannot live without hope' has been proved to be all too true. It was only after a large part of humanity had ceased to believe in the possibility of a 'vertical' progress, the progress of the individual towards the Eternal and Infinite, that men began to fix their hopes on a vague horizontal 'progress' for humanity as a whole towards a state of earthly 'welfare' of which there are many reasons to doubt not merely the possibility but also the desirability—assuming that it is to be the ultimate fruit of the trends now at work—and which in any case no one would ever be free to enjoy for more than a few years, the brief span of human life.

*

The agnostic and the atheist are at liberty to cut off a limb, but they cannot, by refusing to believe in the Transcendent, rid themselves of those psychic elements whose normal function it is to be the vehicles of aspiration towards the Transcendent, and much of the incongruity in the modern world is to be explained by the presence, in the souls of its leaders and others, of quantities of unwanted psychic substance. The danger of this substance being 'at a loose end' is all the greater in that it contains what are, in themselves, the most precious and powerful of the soul's elements; and even apart from atheists and agnostics, the barely lukewarm semi-agnostic religion which characterizes most of those 'leaders of thought' in the modern West who have any religion at all is powerless to open the skylights of the soul and make an outlet for its highest aspirations, which consequently topple over backwards and fall down among the legitimate earthly aspirations, creating there distortion and chaos, and stifling beneath the litter of sentimental and totally unrealistic dreams most of the modest good that sober realism might achieve if left to itself. It is as if a bird, refusing or unable to fly, should be continually tripping itself up with its own wings. Of those virtues which are in fact the wings of the soul, all that remains *(superstat)* of faith is the rigid fanaticism of the pseudo-religion of evolution and progress; all that remains of hope is a ludicrous optimism which struts into the future on minute precarious stepping stones of human 'achievements', many of them exceedingly questionable, across a quagmire of ruin which it refuses to see; and these two superstitions are aggravated by a passionate enthusiasm which invades the mind and which, by being monstrously out of proportion to all its objects, betrays itself as having fallen from the very summit of the soul, and as being in fact the very peak of that summit, the sharp point of man's thirst for the Divine, inverted and turned towards this world where it dissipates all its intensity, dragging the soul through infatuation after infatuation in its vain quest of an earthly Absolute.

FOUR

Freedom and Equality

THE WORLD of today is a chaos of jostling opinions and aspirations. By contrast, the ancient world was always an order, that is, a hierarchy of concepts, each at the level that rightly belongs to it. The chaos has been caused, as we have seen, by the humanistic refusal to recognise anything that transcends the psychic level and by the consequent intrusion of frustrated and perverted other-worldly aspirations into the domain of this world. Equipped as he is by his very nature for worship, man cannot not worship; and if his outlook is cut off from the spiritual plane, he will find a 'god' to worship at some lower level, thus endowing something relative with what belongs only to the Absolute. Hence the existence today of so many 'words to conjure with' like 'freedom', 'equality', 'literacy', 'science', 'civilization', words at the utterance of which a multitude of souls fall prostrate in sub-mental adoration. The superstitions of freedom and equality are not merely the results but also partly the causes of the general disorder, for each in its own way is a revolt against hierarchy; and they are all the more pernicious for being perversions of two of the highest impulses in man. *Corruptio optimi pessima*, the corruption of the best is corruption at its worst; but restore the ancient order and the two idols in question will evaporate from the plane of this world (leaving legitimate earthly aspirations for freedom and equality room to breathe) to take their place once more, transformed, at the very summit of the hierarchy.

The desire for freedom is above all the desire for God, Absolute Freedom being an essential aspect of Divinity. Thus it is that in Hinduism the supreme spiritual state which marks the end of the mystic path is termed deliverance (*moksha*), for it is the state of union (*yoga*) with the Absolute, the Infinite and the Eternal and therefore of freedom from all the bonds of relativity. It was clearly above all to this freedom that Christ referred when He said: 'Get knowledge, for knowledge will make you free', inasmuch as direct knowledge, Gnosis, means union with the object of knowledge, that is, with God. But these words of Christ have also a secondary application at a lower level: there is a relative liberation in indirect knowledge of spiritual truths, for such knowledge means access to a higher world and therefore a possibility of escape from this world. This escape is the 'ascent from the cave' in Plato's famous image, and it will not be out of place to recall here what he says, for it represents the outlook of the ancient world, both Eastern and Western.

Plato—or rather Socrates, for it is into his mouth that Plato puts this discourse[1]—asks us to imagine a large subterranean cave in which are prisoners who have been confined there ever since their childhood. They are made to sit in a long row facing one of the walls of the cave, and they are chained to their seats in such a way that they cannot turn their heads, being only able to look straight in front of them. A fire, raised up behind them, casts its light on to the wall, and between them and the fire puppets are being carried, made in the image of all kinds of living and lifeless earthly creatures. But not being able to turn their heads, the prisoners can only see the shadows which the puppets cast on to the wall in front of them.

Then Socrates tells us to imagine that one of the prisoners escapes from his chains. First he is able to turn round and see the puppets themselves. Then he escapes from the cave and goes up to the outside world where are to be seen all those things in whose likeness the puppets were fashioned. To begin with he is only able to look at their shadows and their reflections in water, first by moonlight and then by sunlight; then he is able to look at the things themselves; and finally he is able to look at the sun.

The cave is this world and the prisoners are mortals during their earthly life. Through lack of objectivity due to inertia, obtuseness and prejudice, the prisoners cannot see clearly even the puppets,

1. Book vii of Plato's *Republic*, or, more correctly, Plato's *State*.

that is, the things of this world; they can only see a vague shadowy likeness of them, 'For now we see through a glass, darkly; but then face to face'.[1] The outside world is the next world, which contains the spiritual realities of which the things in this world are symbols. The increase in the escaped prisoner's powers of vision after he has come up to the outside world corresponds exactly to the increase in the brightness of the smile of Beatrice as she leads Dante up through the seven Heavens. This increase denotes the intensifying of direct intellectual perception as the being rises up throughout the hierarchy of spiritual states, gaining with each a fuller degree of liberation, compared with which the freedom conferred by the escape from the chains seems more and more relative, not to speak of what is commonly called 'freedom', that is, those lesser 'freedoms' such as may be enjoyed by the prisoners themselves, most of whom do not even aspire to be released from their chains. Socrates invites us to imagine how the activities and interests of these prisoners, centred as they are entirely upon the shadows of the puppets, would appear to one who had reached the end of all enlightenment.

If we reflect for a while upon Plato's image, as he certainly intended us to do, it is clear that pre-eminent among those who escape from the cave and then return to it are the Divine Messengers, the founders of religions, some of whom were never prisoners but simply descended from above. In either case their mission is always to tell the inmates of the cave about the sun and the moon, about men and women, animals and birds, trees and flowers, according to their full dimensions, how wonderful they are in shape and in colour; and some of the prisoners drink in their words and are filled with longing to escape from the world of shadows into the real world, but many of them are angry, maintaining that the Prophets are madmen or dreamers, and that the shadows of the puppets are the highest realities that exist.

In the light of this image it will be seen that the difference between the believer and the sceptic is not as the difference between the imprisoned and the free but as between two prisoners, one of whom is conscious of his imprisonment whereas the other refuses

1. I Corinthians 13.

to admit that this world is a prison, because his thoughts stop short at his prison walls.

*

If we now trace the conception of equality back to its source in the Absolute, it will be seen to be an aspect of that supreme spiritual possibility which Christianity calls 'deification' and which Hinduism expresses in the words 'thou art That' (God is thy True Self). The need for equality, which is part of the nostalgia in the soul of fallen man, is above all the need to be 'adequate' once more to the Divine Presence. This adequacy, the greatest of all Mysteries, is expressed in Islam in the words: 'Neither My earth nor My heaven hath room for Me, but the heart of My believing slave hath room for Me.'[1]

The highest Saints are equal in virtue of the equality of their emptinesses which receive the Fullness of the Infinite; and this equality has, underlying its Divine aspect, what might be called a celestial aspect. A mediaeval English poem, *The Pearl*, tells of a man who visits the tomb of his dead daughter and, falling asleep there, has a vision of her in Paradise. He asks her how she is, and she tells him that she is Queen of Heaven. He remonstrates with her, and she replies: 'It is true, as you say, that the Blessed Virgin Mary is Queen of Heaven; but such is her unfathomable kindness and bounty that she allows others to reign as King and Queen beside her.'

Even on the human plane, a society of men who are all 'socially' equal is not merely a utopian dream but a possibility, and tradition tells us that it was in fact the norm on earth for thousands of years. The Golden Age is by definition the age when all men are 'above caste'. But failing such equality, it is clearly better that some elements of humanity should remain relatively excellent than that all should sink to an equal mediocrity, and the 'caste system'[2] was one means

---

1. *Ḥadīth*, that is a saying of the Prophet. These utterances are of two kinds: most of them are termed 'noble' inasmuch as they proceed from the Divine Messenger himself, but a few of them, like the one in question, are 'holy' inasmuch as they are spoken directly by the Divinity upon the tongue of His Messenger.

2. Frithjof Schuon's *Castes and Races* (Sophia Perennis, 1982) throws a long needed light on the whole question of castes and classes according to the different religious perspectives.

among others of safeguarding as far as possible what excellence remained and placing it in a position where it could best benefit society as a whole. This system has moreover amply justified itself, for it was no doubt practised more rigorously and methodically among the Hindus than among other peoples, and it is the Hindus who have succeeded in preserving intact to this day, in all its intellectuality, an exceedingly ancient religion, of which the Greek, Roman and Germanic counterparts were already degenerate in the earliest historic times.

The existence of lower castes, in itself abnormal, is bound to become normal towards the end of a cycle of time, and the ancient world was preoccupied with the problem of self-preservation, how best to stem the tide of degeneration, that is, to check the breeding of inferior human types and lessen the speed of a downward movement which they knew to be inevitable; but the methods of resistance to this movement varied. The caste system implies an acceptance of the fact that a certain degeneration his already taken place. A more ancient means of self-preservation is for a people to hold at arm's length, as the Red Indians do, some of the chief outward causes of human decadence such as the non-nomadic, sedentary life and all that goes with it, and to remain in as close contact as possible with virgin nature, that is, in a physical and psychic contact which is ritualized and illuminated by a truly intellectual contact. This last condition is indispensable.

> It is through the animal species and the phenomena of nature that the Indian contemplates the angelic essences and the Divine Qualities . . ... No object is for them [the Indians] what it appears to be, but it is simply the pale shadow of a Reality. It is for this reason that every created object is *wakan*, holy.
>
> The Red man's sanctuary is everywhere; that is why the earth should remain intact, virgin and sacred, as when it left the Divine Hands—since only what is pure reflects the Eternal. The Indian is nothing of a 'pantheist', nor does he imagine for one moment that God is in the world; but he knows that the world is mysteriously plunged in God.'[1]

1. Frithjof Schuon, *The Feathered Sun*, pp. 67–8.

This perspective imposes a way of life which makes it possible to dispense altogether with a caste system, and to retain a social order which is, at least virtually, a prolongation of primordial equality. There are no 'lower classes' and no 'middle classes' among the Red men; so long as they remain true to themselves and uncontaminated by Palefaces, they are a race of nobles which still produces, in every generation, a small minority of throwbacks to the priest-kings of remote antiquity.

But mere persistence in nomadism, if it is not based on an intellectual contact with nature, is only a safeguard against certain forms of degeneration. There are many different downhill paths, and the world is old enough for some of these to have become widely divergent. The word 'primitive' is used today with far too little discrimination. Compared with men of more primordial ages, the Red Indians of the Iron Age consider themselves degenerate, but relatively speaking they no doubt deserve the title of 'primitive', whereas many if not most 'savages' who are currently called 'primitive' are exceedingly degenerate. There is no sense in calling them primitive simply because a closer contact with nature has saved them from that particular form of decadence which has reached its extreme in the modern civilization.

The incarnation of the intellectual outlook in a strongly constituted spiritual authority is what Plato held to be the best safeguard against decadence, and this is what the Red Indians share with the Hindus as well as with those later sedentary theocracies which have no caste system. Both striking and characteristic are the ways in which the two latest theocracies seek to neutralize or reduce to a minimum the discrepancies between caste and class, that is, between natural qualifications and a social position which is more and more liable to be the result of mere 'accidents'. Christendom retained the existing social order for its partial correspondence to a true caste system but established above it a highest caste which was open to all classes though protected against intruders by the far-reaching sacrifices imposed on its members. In Islam, which is a direct appeal to the priest-king who lies in the depth of man's nature, membership of the highest caste is imposed on all classes; but the gulf between Golden Age ideal and Dark Age fact is bridged by the insistence of the Koran and the Prophet upon 'degrees'. Though it could be misleading to say that the Islamic civilization is pervaded with a sense of caste, it can truly be said that it is outstandingly pervaded with a sense of what is the essence of the caste system, namely a sense of the hierarchy of the different degrees of spiritual possibilities in mankind. Thus, for the Muslim, the secular hierarchy of class distinctions is first of all eclipsed by the virtual equality of priesthood and then replaced by the spiritual hierarchy within the framework of that equality.

In considering how it would be practically possible to form an ideal state, which he calls an 'aristocracy', Plato says that it would first be necessary to find some true philosophers and set them up as rulers, even though it might be against their will. From his description of these aristocrats, it is clear that he means nothing less than Saints in the fullest sense of the word, for the true philosopher is one who has 'escaped from the cave' and has direct vision of the 'sun'. Plato's state is in fact a theocracy: having escaped from the cave, the aristocrat in the full Platonic sense is henceforth able to go to and fro between it and the world above, and here lies the meaning of the function of Pontiff, in Latin *Pontifex*, literally 'bridgemaker'.

But what if the spiritual potentate is far from being in himself a true aristocrat? And has not history shown that the highest offices are liable to be like garments too big for their wearers?

The modern 'solution' is to cut down the garment to fit a dwarf. The way of the ancients was to be patient and hope for a better man. Besides, they knew that the garment itself was precious, even independently of the wearer. The theocrat may be very far from possessing in fact the spiritual degree which corresponds to his function, but that function is none the less itself *pontifex* in the sense that its existence at the head of the state affirms the supremacy of the spiritual above the temporal. It is an official recognition of 'the outlet from the cave' and a guarantee of the collectivity's orientation towards it. Moreover, in addition to the outward hierarchy of spiritual dignitaries there is the inner hierarchy of the Saints, that is, those who are *pontifices* in themselves, independently of any function they may or may not hold, and this inner hierarchy may, practically speaking, replace the outer hierarchy or at any rate throw untold weight into the scales to counterbalance shortcomings in the fulfilment of higher functions. Throughout the Middle Ages Western Christendom had a continuous sequence of great Saints in every generation, men and women whose word was law far and wide, in fact if not in function, and the same is true of the Eastern Church and of the great non-Christian theocracies further East whose 'Middle Ages' have come to an end much more recently. But without the theocratic order itself, with its official outer hierarchy to ensure that the general sense of values is a true one, these Saints could never have 'let their light shine before men' with such dazzling plenitude. Here lies the very point of a theocratic civilization, which only exists in order to further the 'upstream' movement and to check 'downstream' drifting, to set and keep in motion a centripetal impetus which will counteract the centrifugal tendencies of creation—in short, to provide a setting in which religion can best fulfil its function; and the Saints *are* religion, in the sense that they incarnate all that is 'upstream' and centripetal. This applies also by extension to the mystic orders or brotherhoods, each of which is as a prolongation of the life of the Saint who founded it.

In mediaeval Christendom, with its network of monasteries and convents all over Europe and Asia Minor, every village had at least one such centre not very far away, a group of men and women who lived intensely the great cycle of the Christian year—Advent, Christmas, Epiphany, Lent, the Passion, the Resurrection, the Ascension, the Descent of the Holy Ghost, the Assumption of the Blessed Virgin, the Feast of St Michael and all Angels, All Saints, All Souls, linked together throughout the months by the chain of single Saint's day festivals; and the intense living of this cycle set in motion a powerful spiritual vortex into which it was difficult not to be drawn in some measure.

From each centre elementary religious instruction was dispensed to all, and charity to those who needed it. In addition it was always possible for anyone, even the son of the poorest peasant, to receive the very highest instruction, provided that he showed a deep-rooted aptitude worthy of doctrine which itself was rooted in the Spirit. The current notion that 'the lower classes' were 'kept down' in the Middle Ages is based on a purely mundane conception of 'up'. But it would be a contradiction in terms for a theocracy to allow any section of its community to be deliberately hindered from drawing nearer to the Spirit, which is the only mode of rising that a mediaeval monk, for example, would have considered worthy of the name. To him the fact that it was extremely difficult, if not impossible, for the poor to acquire wealth and titles, both of which he himself had turned his back on, would have seemed no great tragedy to say the least. But as to rising in a positive sense, even the most rigid caste system is bound to sanction, at the margin of society, an upward path which is open to all without restriction, including members of the lowest caste.

> If Hinduism considers first of all in human nature those fundamental tendencies which divide man into so many hierarchical categories, it nevertheless realizes equality in the super-caste of wandering monks, the *sannyasis*, in which social origin no longer plays any part. The case of the Christian clergy is similar in the sense that among them titles of nobility disappear: a peasant could not become a prince, but he could become Pope and crown an Emperor.[1]

The individual cases of injustice and oppression, the wide rifts which gaped between theory and practice here and there from time to time in Christendom and in other sacred civilizations known to history were not the fault of theocracy but of the collective decrepitude of the human race in its extreme senility. Moreover, if things went badly, as they very often did, it was thanks to theocracy that they were no worse and that occasionally, at certain times and in certain places, they went well; and there reigned always the hope that what good had happened before would happen again.

The Iron Age as a whole might be called 'the age of the choice between two evils'; the Middle Ages, unlike any subsequent period, had at least the virtue of deserving to be called 'the age of the choice of the lesser evil'. The worst mediaeval Popes and the worst Caliphs of Islam did incomparably less harm than men like Ataturk and other inaugurators of the bleak hopelessness of secularism.

1. Frithjof Schuon, *Castes and Races*, p. 10.

Mediaeval Europe was like a man in the grip of an illness which he knew would prove to be fatal,[1] and which often convulsed his whole body with pain and forced from him groan after groan. But the constitution was sound, the heartbeat was strong and regular. The blood still flowed through the arteries and the veins to the extremities of the limbs; and sometimes the fever would abate for a while, and the patient would remember what it was to possess youth and health. Is it better to be like this or to be, possibly with less suffering, like a body in the last stages of the illness, so drugged that the relatively little discomfort it feels[2] bears no relation to the seriousness of its condition? The heartbeat is scarcely perceptible; the blood almost stagnates in the veins; the skin festers with nauseating eruptions; some outlying parts of the body are already atrophied; and the patient, according to whether he is nearer to coma or delirium, mutters or raves: 'I am getting better and better every day'.

But if it is possible for individuals to fall below the collectivity—though no doubt the word 'below' would not fit every such case, for the depths of misery can be less low than complacence—it is also possible for individuals to escape from the general run in a positive sense. There is no truer proverb than that of the 'ill wind', for it is a metaphysical necessity, resulting directly from the Divine Omnipresence, that there is always a surpassingly good 'best' to be made of every situation. In the present case one aspect of that 'best' might be

1. Our mediaeval ancestors knew well what Plato knew when he said, even of his ideal state (and they were very far from considering their state ideal): 'Everything which is generated is liable to corruption; neither will such a constitution as this remain forever but be dissolved.' Nor would they have been unduly surprised at the turn things have taken this century, for in explaining how his theocracy would inevitably be overthrown and in tracing the stages of degeneration through which the state would pass, Plato mentions 'democracy' and 'dictatorship' as the two lowest possible forms of government, the one tending to lead to the other, 'dictatorship' being, in his conception, the rule of an unprincipled demagogue who is swept into power upon a wave of reaction against the chaos of democracy.

2. Collectively speaking that is; but as regards individuals, the modern world is liable to produce combinations of temperament and circumstance which are impervious even to the strongest 'drugs'. It is not for nothing that our times are often described as 'an age of suicides and "nervous breakdowns"'.

expressed as follows: in the past men proclaimed the vanity of this world actively and directly, voicing the *sauve qui peut* of religion, but the world itself remained relatively silent, whereas now that men are less and less active in proclaiming this truth, the world itself, with men included in a purely passive sense, becomes more and more vociferous of its own vanity. In fact all that we experience daily of a world in its dotage demonstrates that it is indeed a place 'where moth and rust do corrupt', and more and more of the false gods to which men cling are coming to pieces in their very hands.

To say that it is one thing to lose one's faith in this world and quite another to believe in the next is a simplification. We are remotely descended from men for whom there stood, at the boundary between the next world and this, not a closed door but an open one. Their souls were equipped accordingly, and whether we are aware of it or not, we have inherited certain things from them; and though there is no chance that a bird will fly so long as it persists in scraping the earth with its wings, if for some reason it can be induced to stop scraping the earth, there is a good possibility that it will at least attempt to fly.

FIVE

Intellect and Reason

ACCORDING to the doctrine of correspondence between macrocosm and microcosm, the holders of temporal power, that is, the
king and his delegates, are the counterpart in the macrocosm, of the
faculty of reason in the microcosm, whereas the representatives of
spiritual authority correspond to the Intellect. Below the reason
and normally under its control are the faculties of imagination and
emotion and the faculties of sense. In order to exercise its royal
function over these, the reason has need of the priestly sanction
which comes to it from the Intellect, for it depends on the Intellect
for knowledge of the higher principles upon which its government
must be based.

This sanction may come mainly from the outside, that is, from
religion, which has been defined as a partial revelation or exterior-
ization of the Intellect, made necessary by man's loss of contact
with the Intellect within him. The sanction may come also, as in the
case of the true aristocrat, from the re-established inward continuity between the soul, which includes the reason, and the Spirit,
which includes the Intellect. In this case the reason has become
once more, as it was primordially, the projection of the Intellect,
and the connection between the two is one of pure vision. As was
said by a great spiritual authority[1] of the twentieth century:

'Faith is necessary for religions, but it ceases to be so for those
who go further and who achieve self-realization in God. Then one
no longer believes because one sees. There is no longer any need to
believe when one *sees* the Truth.' Between such vision and the lowest
degree of belief there are many intermediary degrees of intuition,

1. Shaikh Ahmad al-'Alawi. See Martin Lings, *A Sufi Saint of the Twentieth
Century* (The Islamic Texts Society, 1993), p. 33.

certainty and faith. The less the outward guidance of religion is corroborated by inward certainty, the more the relationship between reason and Intellect becomes precarious; but provided that it is at least maintained, the soul may be said to possess a third dimension, the dimension of depth or of height.

Three dimensional thought, the only mode of thought that can be considered intellectual, means taking nothing altogether at its face value but always referring it back, along the third dimension, to some higher principle. Ethically speaking, for example, this means always valuing a human virtue as the reflection or symbol of a Divine Quality rather than merely for its own sake. It would be a true definition of sacred art, that is, art in the original conception of it, to say that its function is to reveal or to stress the third dimension in whatever it depicts. Along this dimension, in the light of vision of the spiritual archetypes, or in the lesser lights of various degrees of faith, the authoritative reason is able to interpret the universe to the rest of the soul and to give it its true meaning.

The rationalist is one whose reason refuses to accept the authority of anything higher than itself. Now in the macrocosm, when the temporal power rebels against the spiritual authority, the rebel himself is sooner or later rebelled against. When King James I said 'No bishop, no king', he showed a certain awareness of the universal truth in question. But it was scarcely possible for him, even if he had been so minded, to undo what Henry VIII had done and what had crystallized in the long reign of Elizabeth. The holders of the temporal power in England found themselves as it were fixed in a state of rebellion against the spiritual authority whose function they had usurped, thus sowing the seeds of trouble for their own royal successors. So also in the microcosm, if reason rebels against Intellect, then in their turn imagination and emotion rebel against reason. Having rejected what is above itself, reason is called upon to accept without question all sorts of infra-rational impulses and ends by being not a king but a drudge that is ceaselessly having to work out trains of thought under the dictates of the new tyrants of the soul. The faculty of reason in the humanist, who is the rationalist *par excellence,* is in a situation somewhat analogous to that of the 'constitutional monarch'.

On the other hand if religion, representing the Intellect, demands that man shall accept its authority for all that lies beyond the scope of reason, it never demands that he shall accept what is against reason. The accusations of the humanist to the contrary will not bear examination. For example, the typically rationalistic pretext that since all religions disagree no reasonable man can believe in them is in part simply false, because all religions are in agreement about what is really fundamental, or, in other words, their mysticisms are in agreement; and the pretext is in part unreasonable, because in view of the wide differences between one human collectivity and another it would in fact be strange if Providence were to impose exactly the same religious form on them all.

Far from being irrational, religion always gives man all that can be given in the way of rational grounds for belief, that is, not proof of what could never be made subject to logical demonstration but exceedingly strong 'evidence' of various kinds, both universal and particular; and the reason is invited to sit enthroned in solemn state, with the imagination and the other subordinate faculties attendant upon it, and to give that evidence its very fullest and freest consideration. One such piece of evidence that each religion has to offer is the astounding adequacy of its founder to the exaltedness of his function. A pseudo-religion betrays itself from the start by the incongruous mediocrity of the false prophet in question. By contrast the altogether superlative greatness of the Divine Messenger is such that his absence from history would leave a vast and unimaginable void; and this greatness, with its wide, deep and indelible imprint upon humanity, challenges and defies the mind to explain it otherwise than by allowing that the man in question was, in fact, all that he claimed to be. Apart from its founder, every true religion has also the argument of its lesser lights, men and women of the stature of St Augustine, St Bernard, St Francis, St Dominic, St Catherine of Siena and St Teresa of Avila, to name only a few. The unanimous certainty of such giants, a certainty which infinitely transcends mere belief, is an argument that no truly royal reason will scorn to consider. As to arguments of a different kind, an example which applies in particular to Christianity is the miracle of the stigmata which, since the time of St Francis, has occurred in every generation of

Christians, to at least one or two saintly men or women, until the present day. The humanistic 'explainings away' of these various kinds of evidence are always more or less an insult to reason; and in general, humanism is forever compelling the reason to turn a blind eye to some all-important factor: the evolutionist explanations of the origins of the universe, for example, with their glossing over of the problems of the origin of life and matter, are as sub-rational as the 'psychological' explanations of the origins of religion.

The rationalist thinks by definition in two dimensions only, for his mind is 'free', having 'thrown off the chains of superstition', and these chains, by which reason is tethered to the Intellect, are what make the soul's third dimension. Hence the cult of many conceptions which have in themselves as it were only two dimensions, like statistics, for example, which are so dear to the modern world; and among the experts of two dimensional thought must be counted many of the representatives of so-called 'higher learning'. It is ironical that this term should be used precisely today when increase of knowledge beyond a certain point comes no longer as it used to by 'multiplication', that is, by ennobling length and breadth with the dimension of height, but by 'division', that is, endlessly subdividing a flat surface into more and more minute compartments, in a purely quantitative accumulation of insignificant facts which have escaped the notice—and the interest—of previous generations.

According to the symbolism of the tree which as an image of the universe, microcosm as well as macrocosm, figures in the doctrines of almost all religions, the Spirit is the root of the soul, the reason is its trunk[1] and the other faculties are its branches and leaves. The centrifugal movement to which creation is subject and which means a gradual lessening of contact with the Spirit may then be described as an ever-increasing constriction in the channels through which the sap flows from the root into the trunk, a constriction of which rationalism is a particularly aggravated form. Moreover, the 'sap' has not only an intellectual but also a vital aspect, which means that human

1. Analogously, in the mediaeval science of architecture 'according to some of the Fathers, the holy of holies (in a church) is an image of the Spirit, whereas the nave is an image of the reason' (Titus Burckhardt, *Sacred Art in East & West: Its Principles & Methods*, Perennial Books, 1986) p. 49.

souls tend to be not only more and more loosely knit through weakness of the sinews which bind them together but also more and more stunted through being starved of proper nourishment. This no doubt partly explains one of the differences between earlier and later religions. For while religions are all necessarily the same as regards the essential, that is, as regards man's ultimate need to be reunited with the Spirit, being all infinitely open in an upward direction, it is noticeable that for things which are not essential, Judaism, Christianity and Islam allow man a much less wide 'horizontal' view than Hinduism does, for example. It is as if humanity had been shepherded by religion into a narrower valley than before, with the same vertical opening above but less opportunity for distraction from side to side. We are promised however, that in any case all will be made clear in the next world; and if this used to be enough for most of those it was addressed to, that was because they set the more important above the less important with a sense of proportion forced upon them by the emergency they saw themselves to be in. A man who is fully conscious of being dangerously sick and is promised a permanent cure will not bother over-much as to exactly how he contracted his illness; nor does a man who is making preparations for a journey of no return require to know very much about the country he is leaving. There is no doubt that the telling of lesser truths may sometimes distract the soul from greater truths.

Today, however, such harm as might have been done in the Middle Ages by lesser truths has already been done a thousandfold by other distractions which do not correspond to any kind of truth. The vast cosmological vista of the earlier religions becomes therefore relatively harmless once again—so true is it that 'extremes meet'. Moreover, such a vista is best qualified to meet distractedness on its own ground, so to speak, and to answer some of those questions which overactive minds now tend to ask about religion, while in itself it always remains, at least potentially, what it was in the beginning, a powerful support for meditating on the Infinite.

According to the Hindu doctrines the cycle of four ages which is now nearing its end was preceded by many other such cycles and will be followed by many others; and yet, for all its seemingly endless duration in time, and for all its immensity of spatial extent, our universe is simply one of a countless number of successive worlds through which beings are liable to pass, transmigrating from one world to another upon the rim of the great wheel of the *samsāra*, which is a complete cycle of different states of individual existence; and the *samsāra* upon whose circumference our world is, as it were, one point and one moment is itself simply one of countless *samsāras*, each of which is as a single flash of Divine Manifestation.

The position of a being in any one world is determined by the merit or demerit accumulated in his previous state. What is 'greatly to be desired' and 'hard to obtain' is a central position, for it is only as a member of the central species, which in this world is humanity, that a being has the possibility of escape from the vicissitudes of the *samsāra* and of passing as it were from the circumference along a radius to the Divine Centre. To take this direction is to take 'the way of the Gods' as opposed to 'the way of the ancestors' which means passing on from one samsaric world to another.

The truth of the *samsāra*, with its pre-terrestrial states, is partially expressed in the doctrine of original sin, which serves to single out and stress the essential fact that man is not born into this world in a state of innocence. The same truth is also implicit in the Islamic doctrine that each man's sense of responsibility began when he was created as a seed in the loins of Adam and not merely after his birth into this world.

For a Hindu the doctrine of original sin is self-evident: birth into this world necessarily means imperfection, except in the case of the Divine Messengers, because a being that had reached perfection in a pre-terrestrial state would thereby have already escaped from the *samsāra* altogether. Without sharing this perspective, our ancestors none the less saw that the doctrine of original sin, that is, the doctrine that babies are no longer born into the world as Saints, corresponds to an obvious fact; and indeed this fact could only arouse question in a community which has lost all sense of the human ideal—a community for whom a virtue is no longer required to be, at its best, a dazzling reminder of the Divine Quality which it reflects, but is simply rated according to whether it is more or less beneficial to society, while 'sinlessness' means no more than 'not doing or purposing any harm'.

The post-terrestrial states of the *samsāra* are implicit in what the later religions teach about limbo,[1] and also about hell which corresponds to the sequence of infernal abodes that Hinduism and Buddhism depict in the nethermost section of the samsaric wheel.

Needless to say, these few summary comparisons do not claim to do justice to any of the religious perspectives concerned. Still less do they presume to explain the workings of Providence. But in so far as Providence is prepared to justify Itself for having veiled certain lesser 'horizontal' truths from a section of mankind towards the end of this cycle and for having sought to concentrate all man's diminished energies in a 'vertical' direction, no more eloquent justification could be found than in the history of the Western world for the last two or three hundred years.

It is often said that what has happened was a reaction and that religion is to blame, but this argues a very narrow view of history. The flat 'horizontal' outlook which later came to be known as humanism was already rife in the pre-Christian West and is stamped on almost all north Mediterranean art of two thousand years ago and more. The modern civilization is not merely the death-agony of the Christian civilization. It is also a prolongation of the death-agony of the Greco-Roman civilization which, having been cut short by Christianity, was 'reborn' at the Renaissance. Since then the Western world has remanifested, 'with a vengeance' if one likes to put it that way, its tendency to be distracted from the great truths of the Universe by what it calls 'reality', that is, two-dimensional facts, mainly of a material order.

The circle is a vicious one, since 'freedom', that is, a certain fully achieved degree of distraction, confers on the mind an agility which it did not possess in the past,[2] and this agility opens up possibilities of still further distraction. The ever-increasing facility of travel in the modern world is as an outward image of the ever-increasing

---

1. For this point see Frithjof Schuon, *Etudes Traditionnelles*, 1962, p. 133, note 2.

2. There can be no doubt that men thought more slowly in the past, except for sudden intuitive illuminations, the lightning flashes of the soul, which presuppose some impact of the Intellect. From these the humanist as such is by definition precluded, nor would it be unjust to say that he has preferred, instead, to invent gunpowder, electricity and the like.

glibness and superficiality of the movements of the mind. Despite all the finery of words, what is called 'enriching one's cultural perspective' or 'broadening one's outlook' or 'enlarging one's intellectual horizon' bears no relation to that magnanimity—literally 'greatness of soul'—which is an essential feature of the true aristocrat. If a plastic substance be continually pulled this way and that so as to increase its length and breadth, its third dimension will be reduced to a minimum. The 'broad mind' of the humanist is simply a narrow mind that has been flattened out.

But is it not possible to increase the psychic substance as a whole? The answer to this question is already implied in the image of the tree, for a tree cannot be made to grow by pulling at its branches, and so it is with the soul, whose substance can only receive increase from its root in the Spirit; and if the due performance of rites gives the root of the tree what nourishment it requires, the growth is not only still further encouraged but also made more perfect by the art of pruning, that is, by the abstentions and sacrifices which religion enjoins or recommends.

'In order to take one will surely give first.'[1]

The doctrine of concordant actions and reactions on which Taoism and Buddhism in particular lay emphasis is of such universal importance that it may be considered as the basis of all religious practices. Every action produces a reaction, and as with the waves of the sea, so also if a 'wave' can be made to flow from this world to the next, there will inevitably be an ebb from the next world, and the prescribed rites of a religion are Providence's instructions to man as to how best he may set such waves in motion. The disproportion between the human action and the Divine reaction is so immense that the reaction has to be stored up[2] for the soul in the treasuries of the next world, allowing for an overflow of as much as it is ready to receive in this life.

This question of readiness touches upon the difference between esoterism, which is in itself normal but has become abnormal, and

---

1. Tao Te Ching, Ch. xxxvi.

2. With regard to the Hindu doctrine of 'delayed reactions' see René Guénon, *Introduction to the Study of the Hindu Doctrines* (Sophia Perennis, 1999) pp. 273–76.

exoterism, which is in itself abnormal but has become normal inasmuch as the majority of souls are held in the grip of the Iron Age, this grip being nothing other than the chains of the prisoners in the subterranean cave. The esoteric outlook belongs in this age to those who are in some measure throwbacks to an earlier age, which means a relative looseness in their chains, a foretaste of freedom. But for the majority the chains are too secure to allow them any such foretaste, so that they do not even aspire to escape in this life. If we may borrow Plato's image of our present state to illustrate the teachings of Hinduism and other religions, it may be said that since every rite is conditioned by the aspiration that goes with it, the performance of a rite is in most cases an action of which the reaction is providentially delayed until the great moment of death when the chains are suddenly snapped. At that moment the treasured-up reactions can intervene by giving the prisoner an impetus which enables him to rise to the mouth of the cave and to escape from it, thus taking 'the path of the Gods'. This ascent up to the mouth of the cave corresponds in Christian doctrine—using Dante's image—to the ascent of the Mountain of Purgatory. But without the due performance of rites, that is, without having accumulated the necessary upward impetus, the unchained prisoner could only take 'the path of the ancestors', upon which the very best he could hope for would be to pass on 'horizontally' into the limbo of an adjacent 'subterranean cave'; but if at death the surrounding walls are taken away, so also is the ground from beneath the feet, and religions are in agreement, beneath the diversity of formulations, that failure to take advantage in this life of the privilege of being human—this privilege being the 'talent' that was deposited with each servant in Christ's parable— can scarcely confer any impetus other than a downward one, and that side-stepping 'neutrality' is in fact very rare. 'He that is not with me is against me'; nor was a neutral attitude credited to the servant who gave back no more and no less than the one talent deposited with him.

The escape up from the cave to the outer world after death is salvation in the generally accepted sense of the word, whereas esoterism means that already in this life there is an upward impetus —or more literally an inward impetus, which is symbolically the same; and this impetus is the aspiration to 'grow'. It presupposes firstly the knowledge of what full growth of soul is; and this knowledge, which is shared in a lesser degree also by exoterism, can be strengthened and intensified by concentrated meditation upon the great prototypes of magnanimity. In Christian and Islamic mysticism, for example, respective supports for such concentration are the *Ave Maria* and the invocation of blessings upon the Prophet. A second condition, which is not shared by exoterism, is that the prototype should not be merely a remote ideal but that it should awaken a subjective echo in the soul, a sense of the possibility of actually conforming to it, that is, a sense of the 'looseness of the chains'.

The growth of the soul is a process of alternate contraction and expansion. The performance of a rite may be described from this point of view as a momentary 'lengthwise' and 'breadthwise' contraction of the soul in order to increase its 'height', in the knowledge that the resulting expansion will leave all three dimensions greater than they were before—a broader basis from which to launch a more powerful wave of aspiration.

The regular performance of rites, which alone can bring about a rhythmic ebb and flow between the two worlds, is the basis of every spiritual life, for it is only by maintaining a perpetual 'to and fro' in the channel between soul and Spirit, between mind and Intellect, that this channel can be freed once more from all obstructions.

SIX

The Meeting of Extremes

THE negative tendencies which have been at work in the West for the last few hundred years have become more accentuated, at an always increasing speed, ever since the beginning of the last century. Since then, too, they have been more and more rapidly spreading over the whole face of the globe. But one of the differences between then and now is that the outlook which is responsible for these tendencies, and which seemed so sure of itself, shows signs of wavering. This has not prevented people from continuing to move in exactly the same direction as before, and inasmuch as they are further advanced upon their path the situation is worse; but they are now beginning to move more like helpless automatons than eager enthusiasts, and it is undoubtedly easier for individuals to escape from the general outlook than it was. In the walls of the edifice of the modern world cracks are beginning to gape which were not there before, and these cracks give access to a point of view which represents the very opposite of all that the modern world stands for.

There are many different indications that the present age is drawing towards its close—a close that will be itself the great meeting of extremes—and among these 'signs of the times' are the lesser meetings of extremes which are to be experienced in almost every domain. A striking example of the marked contradiction of the age we live in is that the world has almost certainly never been so rife with pseudo-religions and heresies as it is today, and yet though it is in consequence no doubt easier to go astray than it ever was before, it is at the same time easier to see, among all that goes by the name 'religion', exactly where true religion lies. Beyond the sterile flats of Babism, Bahaism, Christian Science, Theosophy, Anthroposophy,

Moral Rearmament, Subud—to name only a few of this breed—there tower up the great religions of the world—there is no need to mention their names—each like a vast mountain range with its snow-clad peaks of sainthood. Here and there also, in the background, loom the shadowy summits of a more primordial religion which had to be replaced or reaffirmed because its people, having fallen away from it, had forgotten it. But as for a new religion now, there is no room for one in all the world, for there is no longer any people in a state comparable to that of the pre-Christian Greeks, Romans and Germans or to that of the pre-Islamic Arabs, Persians and non-Hindus of India. Every community in the world is now within easy reach, psychologically as well as geographically, of at least one true religion[1] which has remained, despite what heresies may have grown up around it, fully valid and intact, so that it is indeed difficult to conceive of an additional religion being revealed between now and the end of the cycle. Instead, the already existing religions have been as it were renewed and reaffirmed in a time of great need by being given an objective knowledge of each other such as they never had before.

Needless to say our ancestors were aware of the existence of other religions besides their own; but dazzled and penetrated as they were by the great light shining directly above them, the sight of more remote and—for them—more obliquely shining lights on the horizons could raise no positive interest nor did it create problems. Today, however, those horizons are no longer remote; and amidst the great evil which results from all that has contributed to bring them near, some good also has inevitably stolen its way in.

It is true that much if not most of the modern interest in other religions or tolerance of them, far from being based on mutual understanding, is merely the result of academic curiosity or of religious apathy combined with 'the superstition of freedom'. None the less, there are some devout Christians, for example, who need to know, and whose Christian faith is greatly strengthened by the knowledge, that Buddhism is as much a religion as Christianity is,

1. 'This gospel of the kingdom shall be preached in all the world for a witness unto all nations; and then shall the end come.' St Matthew, xxiv, 14.

and that for more than the last two thousand years it has served the spiritual needs of millions of Asiatics far better, presumably, than Christianity could have done. They need to know this because to think otherwise, in their present-day acute awareness of other religions, is to think ill of Providence, and therefore, ultimately, to think ill of Christianity which entirely depends for its glory upon the Glory of God. In more general terms, they need to know, before their souls can be at rest in any one religion, that the Divine Name 'All-Merciful' is no empty word, and that it is not merely one people or one group of peoples that God has 'chosen'; and although it has never been hidden from those who needed to see it, this truth is now probably more accessible than ever before.

It is significant that it was a Pope of our times, and not of any other times, who said to a delegate he was sending to an Islamic country: 'Do not think that you are going among infidels. Muslims attain to Salvation. The ways of God are infinite.'[1]

For some people who have lost or half lost their own religion there is, or can be, a way of return to it through the help of other religions, since it is often easier to look at these objectively and without prejudice; and he who can form a clear idea of what orthodoxy is in any one religion is well qualified to see where its counterpart lies in all religions, including his own, for orthodoxy has a general as well as a particular aspect. As regards particulars, it is not always easy to see how different forms of worship correspond,[2] but in its more general aspects orthodoxy is always fundamentally the same, and one of its most immediately obvious and at the same time far-reaching characteristics is plenitude, in that it fulfils the religious needs of man in every domain and at all the different levels of spiritual qualifications. Here lies one of the chief reasons why no individual can

1. These words, spoken in confidence by Pope Pius xi to Cardinal Facchinetti whom he had just appointed Apostolic Delegate to Libya, were only made public towards the end of the papacy of Pope Pius xii (in *L'Ultima*, Anno viii, 75–76, p. 261, Florence, 1954).

2. Every religion has at least one transcendent element, a descent of the Divine on to the plane of the human, but this element may take different forms. Just as the great heresy in Christianity is to deny the Divinity of 'the Word made flesh' and to deny the prolongation of that Divinity in the Eucharist, so the great heresy in Islam is to deny the Divine Revelation of the Koran, 'the Word made book'.

presume to practise more than one religion, for each religion being 'catholic', that is, being in itself an all-embracing totality, demands a total allegiance which leaves no part of a man free to adhere to anything else.

The Islamic conception of the all-embracingness of orthodoxy is particularly explicit, and from it, leaving aside what concerns Islam alone, we can extract a general definition which might be formulated in the following terms: religion is a threefold Divine Revelation: first, it has a doctrine of what must or must not be *believed* about the Absolute, Infinite and Eternal Truth both in Itself and also as regards the universe, that is, the relative, the finite and the ephemeral, with special reference to man; secondly, it has a law of what must and must not be *done,* and the positive aspect of the law includes a form of worship of sufficient amplitude and variety to enfold and permeate the lives of all the religion's adherents; thirdly, allowing for the wide difference of spiritual gifts among men, it has a mysticism or esoterism. Belief in the doctrine and obedience to the law are binding upon all for they are the means of salvation. The mystical aspect of religion which is only binding upon those who have certain qualifications, is as an extra dimension of faith and worship, for it implies a comprehensive and penetrating grasp of the doctrine and a deep sincerity and concentration in the performance of rites. It offers, beyond salvation, the possibility of sanctification even in this life and, beyond this, the possibility of attaining to God Himself.

Expressed in these general terms, the Islamic conception of the threefold fullness of orthodoxy is clearly too universal not to apply to all other religions also, for it corresponds to undeniable human facts. Nothing of less ample range than this could answer the spiritual needs of any racial or geographical section of the human race as it is today and as it has been throughout 'historic' times;[1] and although the above definition does not touch on particular aspects of orthodoxy, with regard to which each religion must be taken separately, it none the less enables us to see at a glance without going

---

1. Only in ages when mysticism was a norm could it have been said that religion was twofold, consisting simply of doctrine and worship.

into questions of detail, what Churches of Christianity, for example, have remained exempt from the impoverishments which are heresy's chief characteristic,[1] impoverishments of ritual and doctrine which amount to an elimination of mysticism altogether, for mysticism being an enrichment or ennoblement of the rites and the doctrine is in this sense the very antithesis of heresy. The same truth might be expressed by saying that mysticism accepts with the fullest understanding all that heresy rejects through insufficient understanding.

Religions may be likened in their outward or exoteric aspects to different points on the circumference of a circle and in their esoteric or mystical paths to radii leading from these points to the one centre which represents the Divine Truth. This image shows exoterism as the necessary starting point of mysticism, and it also shows that whereas the different exoterisms may be relatively far from each other, the mysticisms are all increasingly near and ultimately identical, converging upon the same point.

Men have always had access to the testimony not merely of believers in Divine Truth but of eye witnesses to It, namely the Saints of their own particular religion. But now, as it were to compensate for the general cult of scepticism, this testification to the Absolute, the Eternal and the Infinite through direct experience of Oneness with God has been made more irresistible than ever, for those who are prepared to listen to it, through being corroborated by a multitude of other voices on every horizon, the voices of the Saints of other religions, testifying to the same supreme possibility for man, and by extension to the truth of religion in general, with its doctrine that the things of this world are merely the shadows of higher realities.

1. With regard to the widely deplored impoverishments which have taken place in Roman Catholicism since the Second Vatican Council—impoverishments staunchly resisted by a faithful few—it is enough to state the astonishing facts as they are. One of them is that the heads of the Church suddenly decided to abolish and to forbid the use of the traditional liturgy on which every member of the Church had been brought up and which was thus the basis of the spiritual life of millions of men and women. Comment is unnecessary. But those who wish to be informed of other facts and how it all came about should see Rama P. Coomaraswamy, *The Destruction of the Christian Tradition* (Sophia Perennis, 1981). See also Appendix Two and in *The Eleventh Hour* (Archetype, 2001), Appendix c.

If it can be said that man collectively shrinks back more and more from the Truth, it can also be said that on all sides the Truth is closing in more and more upon man. It might almost be said that, in order to receive a touch of It, which in the past required a lifetime of effort, all that is asked of him now is not to shrink back. And yet how difficult that is!

Religions are quite explicit about the great compensations for the difficulties of the Dark Age, and these compensations are bound to be more and more marked as the age draws to its close. According to the parable of the workers in the vineyard, those who came to work only a short while before sunset received the same wage as those who had worked hard during the heat of the day; and the Prophet of Islam said: 'Verily ye are in an age in which if ye neglect one tenth of what is ordered, ye will be doomed. After this a time will come when he who shall bserve one tenth of what is now ordered will be saved.'

This does not imply, however, that anything short of perfection could ever pass through the gate of Paradise. In Hinduism the Vishnu-Purana does not say that less virtue is required of men today but that 'in the Dark Age men can achieve the highest virtue by a very small effort'. Similarly, the Prophet said that the Muslim's five daily canonical prayers are sufficient, not in themselves, but because they are counted by God as being equal to fifty of the prayers of the men of old.

What is positive in the present time is that with regard to the cycle as a whole it represents completeness and finality: only when it has brought to fruition all the different possibilities which were latent in it at its outset can the cycle come to an end; only then can the macrocosm, the outer world, be 'rolled up like a written scroll', to give place to 'a new heaven and a new earth'. The same is true, analogously, in the microcosm, the little world of the individual soul; it is only when the soul has succeeded in integrating all its elements that it can 'die' and that a new and perfect soul can be 'born'. To achieve this 'death' and 'rebirth', either before or after the death of the body, is the aim of all spiritual practice for, 'Except a man be born again, he cannot see the kingdom of God'.[1] But every true cosmos has a centre,

1. St John, III, 3.

and it would no doubt be true to say that most souls today are too disintegrated, too unaware of the centre within them, to count as microcosms. They have as it were lost their identity, having been swallowed up by the macrocosm where their function is the merely fragmentary one of representing various possibilities of human decadence. But if a soul can extricate itself from the macrocosm and make itself into something of a microcosm once more by means of religion which confers on it at least a virtual contact with its centre, or in other words if a soul has the strength to re-establish itself virtually as a little world side by side with the big world, then it can benefit, by a kind of refraction, from all that is positive in the state of the big world. The finality and completeness of a macrocosm which is racing towards its end will help to precipitate finality and completeness in the microcosm, causing the soul to 'run to seed' in a purely positive sense; and since this is also, concurrently, the effect of sacred rites, whose purpose is to bring the soul to fruition, it may be said that the rites 'count' more than they did because to the power that they have in themselves is harnessed the impetus of the times.

If the workers in the vineyard all received the same wage it was because the latecomers, owing to a providential difference of conditions, were in fact able to gather in a small space of time just as much fruit as those who had worked throughout the heat of the day.

Appendix One

This appendix has been added to the second edition for the benefit of those who might like to have more information about one of the books on evolutionism referred to in Chapter 1, *The Transformist Illusion* by Douglas Dewar (Sophia Perennis, 1995). The author treats his subject from many different angles—physical, geological, palaeontological, geographical and biological—his method being always to present us with the facts and to draw a sharp line of demarcation between fact and theory—a line which evolutionists have done all they can to blur. Particularly significant in this respect is a chapter on 'Alleged Fossil Links between Man and Non-Human Ancestors', which makes it clear that there exist fossils of men of modern type which are far older than those of 'Pekin man' and other supposed 'missing links'.

Equally instructive in its own way is the chapter which follows this, 'Transformism versus the Geological Record'. The geological evidence is hostile to the theory of evolution while at the same time it in no sense contradicts the religious doctrine of sudden creation for, as Dewar has pointed out in an earlier chapter, 'the abruptness with which new Classes and Orders of animals make their first appearance in the rocks known to us is one of the most striking features of the geological record'. Unable to turn an altogether blind eye to this, some of the more objective evolutionists have sought to save evolutionism and at the same time to avoid having recourse to a Divine Creator, by endowing nature herself with powers of sudden creation which are termed 'explosive evolution' (Schindewolf) or *aramorphosis* (Severtzoff and Zeuner). Such theories have the added convenience of absolving the evolutionist from the need to produce missing links.

'Schindewolf ... asserts that it is useless to look for missing links in many cases, because the supposed links never existed. The first bird hatched from a reptilian egg.'

No less miraculous, however, are the gradual changes imagined to have taken place by the 'non-explosive' evolutionists, whose texts continually rely, not without success, on the ignorance of the layman or on his lack of observance. Dewar gives many outrageous examples of such exploitation, from amongst which we may quote Darwin's remark: 'With some savages the foot has not altogether lost its prehensile power, as is shown by their manner of climbing trees and of using them in other ways', and since a point of central significance is touched on here, we should be justified in dwelling on it for a moment attentively—more attentively than Darwin would have wished, for he must have been well aware of the following facts. Any normal human being can develop with practice, if driven by circumstances, certain powers of grasping with the feet. But such development can be only within very narrow limits, for organically the human foot, unlike the human hand, is not made for grasping. It is made to serve as a basis for man's upright posture and gait, whereas the foot of an ape is organically as prehensile as a hand. In the human foot the transverse ligament binds together all five toes, whereas in the ape it leaves the big toe free like a thumb. Now let any reader look at his own hand, which in the above respect is similar to the foot of an ape, and ask himself whether it is imaginable that even in millions of millions of years the ligament that binds together the four fingers could ever come to throw out a kind of noose, lassoo the thumb, and bind it up together with the fingers, all this, presumably, taking place under the skin. When Darwin says 'the foot has not altogether lost its prehensile power' does he mean 'the lassooing has already taken place but the roping in has not quite been effected'? But he relies on such questions not being asked.

Another way of taking advantage of the layman is through terminology, and in this connection Dewar fully confirms a suspicion that some of us have already had, the suspicion that under cover of technical terms scientists sometimes talk or write nonsense with impunity. A case in point, given in the chapter on 'Some Transformations Postulated by the Doctrine of Evolution', is an account by

Dr R. Broom, an authority on the fossils of the South African mammal-like reptiles, of how he supposes the mammals to have evolved from the Ictidosaurians. In Broom's own language the account sounds quite impressive though it is more or less unintelligible to the layman. Translated by Dewar into plain English, it reads:

> Some reptile scrapped the original hinge of its lower jaw and replaced it with a new one attached to another part of the skull. Then five of the bones on each side of the lower jaw broke away from the biggest bone. The jaw bone to which the hinge was originally attached, after being set free, forced its way into the middle part of the ear, dragging with it three of the lower jaw bones, which, with the quadrate and the reptilian middle-ear bone, formed themselves into a completely new outfit. While all this was going on, the Organ of Corti, peculiar to mammals and their essential organ of hearing, developed in the middle ear. Dr Broom does not suggest how this organ arose, nor describe its gradual development. Nor does he say how the incipient mammals contrived to eat while the jaw was being rehinged, or to hear while the middle and inner ears were being reconstructed!

Broom's hypothesis is not just an exceptional freakish vagary, but a typical example of the sort of transformation that the evolutionist assumes to have been repeated again and again all along the line of any existing animal's evolution from the first 'one-celled' ancestor. What is exceptional in Broom's case, is that unlike most others he does at least try to explain how the supposed transformation might have occurred. Dewar comments, not without justice:

> One reason why the evolution theory was so readily accepted was the belief that, while the theory of special creation involves the miraculous, that of evolution does not. One of the aims of the present book is to demonstrate that the theory of evolution, far from dispensing with miracles, involves more than does the theory of creation. Meantime, most people are altogether ignorant of this and other equally significant facts that *The Transformist Illusion* lays bare. One result of this ignorance is the flood of

books by non-scientists about the history of mankind, books for adults and books for children, which take evolution altogether for granted, as a truth that no reasonable man would call in question, and which pour out, year after year, doing untold harm; and not the least harmful of these books are those by believers on the brink of unbelief, some of them religious dignitaries, who seek to stabilize their own and others' tottering faith by a reinterpretation of religion in conformity with 'the light of modern scientific knowledge.'

*

Looking at the question from a different angle, one which is more in the spirit of the book to which this appendix has been added, it must be remembered that only by escaping from time can man escape from the phases of time. The spiritual path escapes from these phases because only its starting point lies altogether within time. From there onward it is a 'vertical' upward movement through domains which are partly or wholly supratemporal as represented in Dante's *Purgatorio* and *Paradiso*. But modern science does not know of any such movement, nor is it prepared to admit the possibility of an escape from the temporal condition. The gradual ascent of no return that is envisaged by evolutionism is an idea that has been surreptitiously borrowed from religion and naively transferred from the supra-temporal to the temporal. The evolutionist has no right whatsoever to such an idea, and in entertaining it he is turning his back on his own scientific principles. Every process of development known to modern science is subject to a waxing and waning analogous to the phases of the moon, the seasons of the year, and the different periods of man's life. Even civilizations, as history can testify, have their dawn, their noon, their late afternoon and their twilight. If the evolutionist outlook, instead of being sectarian and pseudo-religious, were genuinely 'scientist' in the modern sense, it would be assumed that the evolution of the human race was a phase of waxing that would necessarily be followed by the complementary waning phase of devolution; and the question of whether or not man was already on the downward phase would be a major feature of evolutionist literature. But the question is never put. Nor can there be any doubt that if evolutionists could be made to face up to it, most of them would drop their theory as one drops a hot coal.

There could be no question of any such evolution from the standpoint of ancient natural science, which did not claim to have everything within its scope, that is, within the temporal domain, and could therefore admit to being transcended by the origins of earthly things. For those origins, it looked beyond temporal duration to the Divine creative act which places man (and the whole earthly state) on a summit from which evolution, in the sense of terrestrial progress, is inconceivable.

Appendix Two

The Destruction of the Christian Tradition, referred to on page 65, note 1, gives a brilliantly written and fully documented account of what took place immediately before, during and after the Second Vatican Council. The author is above all concrned with what is orthodox and what is heretical, and his altogether clear, direct and simple treatment of his subject is based on the decisions of previous councils and the pronouncements of the greatest authorities of the Church throughout the centuries. What he has written is self suffi-cient and needs no additions. But from a slightly different angle, and as it were to meet the modernists on their own ground which is that of psychic expediency, we will nonetheless add here the following remarks.

Those responsible for the changes in question have pleaded that a religion must conform to the times, to which it must be answered: Not if to conform means to cease to be itself, and to become the accomplice of the times. But true conformity is different: medicine, for example, in order to conform to an age, must be capable of sup-plying antidotes to all that is most prevalent in the way of illness. Analogously, it would not be unreasonable to maintain that in order to conform to an age characterized by drastic change and turbulent unrest, religion should be more than ever ready to display, and even to advertise, the rock-like stability without which, as a vehicle of Eternal Truth, it can never in any case be true to itself. There is no doubt that the human soul feels a deep need for something in its life which will always remain the same, and it has the right to expect its religion to be the unfailing constant which fulfils this need.

Such considerations as these were thrown to the winds by the Second Vatican Council. It is therefore not surprising that it should have precipitated an unparalleled crisis, and the gravity of the situation can be measured to some extent by the following figures. Between the years 1914 and 1963 the Catholic Church received only 810 requests from priests to be allowed to relinquish their priesthood, and of these requests only 355 were accepted. During the first fifteen years after the council there were over 32,000 defections from the priesthood. These figures must be taken to refer partly to the culprits of the crisis and partly to its victims; and as to the victimization, which concerns both clergy and laity, it is significant that the traditional liturgy has not merely been discouraged but even expressly forbidden. The strategy would fail altogether but for the fact that the vast majority of laymen—and this applies also in a certain measure to the clergy themselves—are under the illusion that the obedience which they owe to the clerical hierarchy is absolute. One of the great merits of Rama Coomaraswamy's book is that it shows clearly at what point, according to strictly traditional Catholic doctrine, obedience becomes a sin, and at what point authority, even that of a Pope, becomes null and void.